FAREWELL
TO THE
HORSES

FAREWELL
TO THE
HORSES

DIARY OF A BRITISH TOMMY
1915–1919

ROBERT ELVERSTONE

The
History
Press

'Dedicated to the memory of my sister Margaret Anne Taylor (née) Hoyte,
who was the niece and god-daughter of Cady Cyril Hoyte.'

Barbara Hoyte

First published 2014

The History Press
The Mill, Brimscombe Port
Stroud, Gloucestershire, GL5 2QG
www.thehistorypress.co.uk

British Library Cataloguing in Publication Data.
A catalogue record for this book is available from the British Library.

ISBN 978 0 7509 5222 4

Typesetting and origination by The History Press
Printed in Great Britain

CONTENTS

ACKNOWLEDGEMENTS

I would like to thank Cady's niece, Barbara Hoyte, for allowing me to share this important historical document with a wider audience and for help with detail and research.

Thanks also to the staff of the Chilvers Coton Heritage Centre, Avenue Road, Nuneaton, for help with research and technical details, especially to Rob Everitt for a very interesting and informative tour of the centre.

The photographs, unless specifically indicated otherwise, have all been used by permission of the Hoyte family and have been taken from the family photograph album.

Finally, thanks must go to Cady Hoyte for the foresight to share his experience and for the sacrifices that he, and many more like him, made when he agreed to accept the 'King's Shilling'.

'My sincere thanks to Robert Elverstone, for all his interest, enthusiasm, technical expertise and many hours of work, without which this diary would never have been published.' – Barbara Hoyte

FOREWORD

July 28th 1914 is remembered as the day war was declared in Europe. Young men, from all walks of life, either joined voluntarily or were conscripted to fight in what they thought was to be a short conflict to defend freedom and democracy. Many believed the fighting would be over in a short time and that they would be home for Christmas. The reality was to prove very different.

On 28 June 1915, Warwickshire-born Cady Cyril Hoyte, aged 19, joined the Machine Gun Corps of the Warwickshire Yeomanry (the Warwicks). Leaving his home town of Nuneaton behind, Private 164684 Hoyte was sent to Tidworth Training Camp before being shipped to Egypt, where he fought as part of the British Expeditionary Force.

After the fall of Gaza, Cady was then sent to fight in the trenches of Northern France. Shipped aboard the *Leasowe Castle*, Cady was a survivor of the German U-boat torpedo attack which sunk the stricken vessel, before being transported across Italy by train, finally to arrive in France.

Throughout his time with the British Army, Cady kept a diary detailing not only the fears and horrors of the fighting, but also the ordinary daily events of army life. He writes with particular fondness of the horses with which he develops not only a working relationship, but also a true love of these magnificent animals that carried their riders to battle and, so often, to death.

At the end of the war, Cady began to type his diary in the form of a narrative, detailing his entire army career from inception to his final demob in February 1919. He writes with an easy narrative and humour, but never loses sight of his respect for human life and the friends he makes, and loses.

Throughout the diary, the horses are never far from Cady's thoughts. The reader understands and is able to empathise with Cady when the time comes to say farewell.

It was by chance that I heard about the diary when researching material for another book. Barbara Hoyte, who is Cady's niece, had inherited the transcript and kept it safely tucked away in a cupboard. What a fortunate moment, when over a welcome cup of tea I was asked, 'Would you like to read it?'

In transcribing this version of the diary, I have made minor changes to the original script with the intention of making the narrative more easily readable. The detail, dates, description and historical content remain unchanged and can confidently be used as the basis for further historical research.

INTRODUCTION

Perhaps it is necessary to briefly summarise the period immediately preceding the time of the opening of the following diary; which is not intended to be in any way a record of the war, but merely the jottings of a common British Tommy who, prior to August 1914, had no thoughts or ambitions of shouldering a rifle in the service of his King and Country. Having metaphorically received the King's Shilling and a new suit of khaki, the immediate introduction to the wilds of Salisbury Plain marked the commencement of real military life.

Here the soft corners of civilian life were soon knocked off, and all signs of individuality sunk beneath the title of an official regimental number. One quickly learned the difference between a 'full-blown' sergeant major and a temporary, acting, unpaid lance corporal; the former being easily recognisable by two things – the crown on his sleeve and his astounding vocabulary. From the latter, it was very evident that 'damn' was not swearing but merely the means of expressing oneself in the briefest but most effective manner.

Little time was required to learn the precise meaning of such expressions as fatigue, clink, CB, canteen (both varieties), and such orders as, 'Fall in the guard', 'Prepare to mount', 'Cross your stirrups', or even to unblushingly meet such shafts of sarcasm as, 'Slacken your reins or you'll give your horse the headache!' and, after an all-too involuntary fall, 'Who gave you the order to dismount?'

Then, too, by hours of monotonous instruction, one was taught the difference between a gun and a rifle; between a horse's off fore fetlock and its near hock; and that, when on guard, to move about in a smart and soldier-like manner and to challenge all persons approaching one's post between sunset and reveille.

All this brought us up to the time when the riding school instructor (an old regular who had won his rough-riding spur) administered his final words of advice: 'When you get out yonder there are three things to remember; Number One first; Number One second; Number One third and, if there is a fourth, then Number One fourth' – a very forcible way of explaining that it would be a case of every man for himself.

At any rate, by this time we figured that the result of our training could be aptly summed up as follows: 'To kill is your duty, but to be killed is damned bad luck!'

Up to this point our daily routine had been somewhat as follows:

Reveille: 6 a.m.

Roll call: 6.10 a.m. followed immediately by 'stables' for the purpose of mucking out, in which process no shovels were allowed; hands were made before shovels in the eyes of the military authorities.

Breakfast: 7 a.m. after which we had to wash, shave and clean our buttons and boots before parading at 7.30; those for riding school in breeches and putties, and the remainder in slacks (fatigue dress).

As I was on transport, the whole morning was spent in drawing forage and rations from the supply dump near the station. After dinner, at one o'clock in the afternoon, we had to change into riding breeches and putties, saddle-up our horses and parade for riding school at two o'clock. (Some of our early struggles with saddle and horse can very well be left to imagination.) On returning from riding school (two hours of it), we had to water and rub down our horses, then hurriedly change again into slacks and parade for musketry at half past four. This lasted until teatime at six o'clock, for which we were allowed half an hour; then parade again for an hour's lecture, sometimes on discipline, other times on map reading, or on the 364 parts which go to form a horse.

After this there would be a good hour's work on saddle cleaning, which brought the day to a close, but a few short hours before the same thing commenced all over again. It will therefore, I think, be readily understood that our opinion of Tidworth was far from a flattering one.

1

1915 – TIDWORTH TRAINING CAMP

— November 9th —

On this typical November morning I was sent back to the military hospital at Tidworth to be formally discharged, after having spent the past fortnight, very enjoyably, at a convalescent home in the little Wiltshire town of Pewsey. The cause of my visit there had been a badly poisoned knee, which was really the result of a rather severe boil which, in its turn, was due to the army rations. Having apparently found a warm corner in the heart of the matron at Pewsey, the good lady had given me a written recommendation for five days' sick leave. So it was with a light heart, and a somewhat stiff knee, that I faced the medical officer at Tidworth who reported me fit for light duty. Now I strode as briskly as possible across the barrack square, my kitbag feeling no heavier (in spite of my stiffness) than the purse in my pocket, whose weight may be judged from the fact that I had not seen a pay day for rather more than three weeks.

With but one brief halt to make sure that my recommendation paper was safe in my pocket, I made a beeline for the orderly room and, having such faith in that scrap of paper, I already pictured myself comfortably ensconced in the afternoon train to London and civilisation.

By this time, I was on the threshold of the orderly room and, unhesitatingly, knocked on the door. It was immediately opened by the sergeant major himself, who greeted me with, 'Well Hell! So you've come back to work again at last.'

Not a very encouraging opening, but I replied, 'Well Sir, my knee is not quite right yet. In fact, I was told to present this to you.' And I handed over the precious slip of paper. (You will observe how thoroughly I had learnt the noble art of 'spinning the yarn' diplomatically, for one had to be most diplomatic in their dealings with sergeant majors.) While he perused it, I tried to look like a wounded soldier, hoping that might help to soften his heart, if indeed sergeant majors were blessed with such organs. I soon decided they were not, for after one glance at his face I said goodbye to the thoughts of trains, refreshment rooms and everything else appertaining to civilisation, and felt that I was already on the way to the front line.

'A damn nice thing this,' he broke out. 'After five days' leave, and three weeks in hospital, you have the cheek to come back here and ask for another leave. You're in the army now, my lad, and you've come back to work. Report yourself to the sergeant at Number 2 Stable and he will find you a job.'

At this point I was quite prepared to believe all the horrid things I had heard of sergeant majors in general and, without giving view to my own views, I concluded that to say the least they were not nice people to know.

Fearing that more severe imprecations might follow if I remained, off I went in the direction of Number 2 Stable ... but no! I would not report there. Damn the sergeant and his job. Consequently, with a feeling of strong defiance, I turned my steps towards the YMCA hut and squandered the major portion of the contents of my purse in a cup of tea and some biscuits.

Here I remained until a convenient moment presented itself to make my way unseen to the dining hall for dinner. After mapping out and following a zigzag course, I was just beginning to breathe freely again in sight of my objective when, in rounding the last corner, I ran slap bang into the afore-mentioned sergeant major. My knees began to weaken and I walked with a decided limp (a happy idea) as I continued my way, for there was no possible chance of escape.

Fortunately I was just opposite the stable where I was supposed to have been so diligently at work during the past hour and a half. No doubt the sergeant major thought I had just completed my task. However, as I had already decided that he was quite devoid of that organ usually associated with mothers and lovers, I was quite prepared for all that followed: in his best parade voice, the sergeant major shouted, 'Hi there! Go to Number 1 Stable and relieve the stable guard while he has his dinner.'

Being fairly convinced that discretion was the better part of valour, I obeyed his order with alacrity.

During a period that seemed to last for hours, I pushed a barrow up and down that stable, the cause of my labours forcing me to the conclusion that army horses were being fed altogether too well. As the time dragged on I decided that the food for the troops must have greatly improved in quantity, if not in quality, during my absence in hospital.

At last I was relieved but found no appetite for the grub which met my eyes as I entered the dining hall. The excellent food I had received during the past few weeks put me off the food now before me, and besides, the disappointment at not getting my leave granted was enough in itself to put any chap off his food.

So I again sought refuge in the YMCA where, after making use of their stationery to write several letters, I became quite reckless and spent my few remaining coppers on more tea and biscuits. At any rate, I had no money left to worry about now. Therefore I knew at teatime that I must eat whatever was provided or go without altogether, and it did not take long to come to a decision. After tea, the hours dragged wearily along until, eventually, I put down my blankets and got into bed.

The next morning, the very unwelcome sound of reveille served to renew the bitter disappointment of the previous day and so, in a half-hearted sort of manner, I shuffled down to roll call determined to 'swing the lead' to the best of my ability. This I did fairly effectively but, at eleven o'clock – the time the morning post was due – I piloted myself to the post room, but came away disappointed as there was nothing for me.

I managed to pass away the time until the afternoon post arrived, when I again made my way to the post room. This time I was amply rewarded, for there was a registered letter in addition to those letters I had expected. This immediately put new life into me and, at that moment, I felt that I didn't care a 'tinker's cuss' for all the sergeant majors in the whole British Army, and decided to treat myself to a seat at the garrison theatre that night.

With tea over, I paid quite a lot of attention to my toilet before setting off to the theatre where, after spending some considerable time in the queue, I eventually secured a seat in the gallery.

A number of variety turns, followed by a sort of revue composed chiefly of gaudily but scantily clad chorus girls, helped to pass away a fairly pleasant evening so that I returned to barracks in a rather more cheerful mood.

November 11th

Today passed by quite uneventfully, except that in the evening I paid another visit to the theatre and, from my seat in the gods, I spotted my old pal the sergeant major in one of the seats down below. Had he been aware of all that was passing through the mind of a certain individual up in the gods, he would not have sat there so serenely.

November 12th

After roll call, a party of our men, who had been detailed for a draft for overseas, were granted their five-day draft leave. During the morning, as I watched these men march off to the station, my own disappointment was renewed.

In the afternoon, however, I was ordered to report to the orderly room, and it was with a feeling half of fear and half of defiance that I obeyed the order. Upon arrival, the sergeant major called me to enter and I was surprised at the unusually friendly note in his voice, causing me to wonder whether after all he had succeeded in finding, somewhere in his anatomy, something in the nature of a heart.

To cut a long story short, he wanted to know whether I was sure I was fit enough to 'stand to' for an overseas draft. He went on to explain that, after the original draft men had proceeded on leave that morning, he had received an order that they were to leave for Plymouth the following day, and consequently he had had to wire for them all to return to barracks immediately.

As it was doubtful whether they would all get back in time, he had to detail other men to be ready to take their places. Being absolutely fed up with the army generally, and being more anxious still to get out of the grip of the person I was now facing, I assured him that I was as fit as could be and that my knee was perfectly well again. My name was duly entered on the draft roll and excitement quickly overcame my previous 'fed-upness'.

As I had but recently returned from hospital, I was deficient of quite a lot of necessary equipment, and as a result spent the next few hours rushing backwards and forwards between the quartermaster's stores and the barrack room, until I was finally re-equipped as far as possible.

As the evening wore on, draft men began to return from leave, each voicing his own grievance at being called back; in some cases, the wire ordering his return had arrived before the individual himself. That night, we were all excited and few slept, as draft men were straggling back into barracks almost all through the night. As I lay awake, I hoped against hope that someone would still be absent in the morning, for my whole mind was now set on going 'out yonder'.

— November 13th —

Before dawn, reveille was sounded and, at roll call, it was ascertained that three of the men of the original draft were still absent. It was now certain that I would be going the first part of the journey at least.

We paraded immediately after roll call, and after the colonel and the sergeant major had bid us farewell, the band of the 4th and 7th Dragoon Guards struck up, and in the cold grey dawn, we marched off to the station.

Tidworth being purely a military camp, the first stage of our journey was certainly not in the nature of a triumphal procession through flag bedecked streets. However, a small band of staunch pals accompanied us to the station and, as our train moved off, gave us a final cheer and a shout of good luck.

Little need be said of the journey to Plymouth. As the surrounding country flew past us, there were many half-unconscious sighs heaved at the thought that this was probably our last view of home; not literally, but England was home, and what could have been more fitting than our last glimpse being one of glorious Devon.

On arrival at St Budeaux Camp, Plymouth, we were allotted billets in a large wooden hut; tea was served and we were issued with passes permitting us to be out of camp until, I believe, eleven o'clock. As all my most intimate pals had gone out on an earlier draft – while I was in hospital – I now wandered alone, almost aimlessly, through the streets of Plymouth, finally taking refuge in a cinema. The pictures held little interest for me, however, as I sat and wondered what the folks at home would think when they heard that, instead of going home on leave, I was already on the way out to take my place in the 'great and glorious adventure'. Of this latter fact I was truly proud and, in spite of my present loneliness, was determined that nothing should now prevent my continuing the journey onwards.

— (Sunday) November 14th —

Today we were not allowed out of camp. Instead, we were issued with rifles and swords, along with a dozen other things, in order put the final touches to our overseas kit.

The soaking wet day eventually drew itself to a close and the majority, after writing our farewell letters, felt that we were quite ready.

Two of the men who had been absent when we left had now rejoined us, which meant that two of the three who had taken their places were to return to Tidworth. The sergeant major had sent word that I was to have the first chance to go back, but I was determined that should not be, and so it was settled that I would go on with the draft – and so ended my last night in England.

2

DISEMBARKATION
– HMS *CALEDONIA*

Early in the morning, the whole camp was bustling as everyone was preparing for the march to the docks. Our little party, about thirty in all, moved off at about half past nine in the morning, and this time it was rather more in the nature of a procession, as flags fluttered from the windows of almost all the houses on the route. As we marched along, women and children leaned out of the windows and cheered us, but in many cases it was noticed that the handkerchief held out to wave goodbye was rapidly withdrawn to dry a tear.

Around midday we marched up the gangway on to HMS *Caledonia*, which was to carry us to our unknown destination. Having stowed our rifles and been allocated messes, we all went up on deck to take a long, last look at England. Now, for the first time, I almost wished I had taken my chance of returning to Tidworth, but regrets were now of no avail and, realising that, I ran below and scribbled a hasty message home which I asked a sailor on shore to post for me.

As daylight faded and lights sprang up all around, the boat moved from her moorings and a very heavy load settled around my heart as I realised that our last actual link with England was now severed.

For some considerable time I paced the deck in company with another man of our draft, our eyes glued on the lights ashore as, one by one, they gradually disappeared. As the last flickered out, I became aware of a feeling of despair, for it seemed that we were now left to face the unknown absolutely alone.

It soon grew chilly and so we went below to prepare our hammocks for the night. Down here a good many hammocks were already slung. The thumping of the ship's engines were so loud and regular that they merely added to that feeling of despair.

— *November 16th* —

I awoke early but could not say that I had had an altogether pleasant night in this strange bed amidst such strange surroundings. The atmosphere was hot and stuffy and the hammocks slung so close together that there was hardly room for them to swing with the motion of the boat.

The first thing I heard on waking was talk of bread, butter and jam, and I found that these commodities had already been drawn for our mess, and that the two mess-orderlies were already on their way to the cookhouse to draw the porridge and bacon for breakfast. As a good soldier always has a good appetite in spite of his surroundings, I immediately began to prepare for breakfast as the others were doing.

Having all squeezed round the table – eighteen men at a table constructed for fourteen – the arrival of the tea was haled with joy and there was soon a clang of tin mugs as they were passed to the end of the table to be filled. After waiting some time for the arrival of the porridge, during which period our hunger was intensified by the sight of men at the other messes eagerly scoffing theirs, one of our men went to find out what was happening – he soon found the missing orderly leaning over the side of the boat in quite an unfit state.

During the morning, both our orderlies were seized with a very earnest concern for the welfare of the fish and, by evening, the greater part of our little company was paying toll to Neptune. My new-found pal and I, being about the only two men to remain alright, undertook the duties of mess orderlies for the remainder of the voyage.

— *November 17th* —

Only a very small number of us were now in a fit state to come below at meal times, and you may guess that we lived nobly up to the standard of a soldier's appetite.

On the following morning we had to parade before the medical officer (MO), roll up our sleeves and receive the stamp of his inoculating needle. This put paid to several other men who had been hovering dangerously on the borderline of *mal-de-mer*.

By this time, the large circle of water all around us was becoming tedious, and the never ceasing swish of the water churned up by the ship's bows, especially at night when no lights were allowed, sounded somewhat dismal and uncanny.

— *November 19th* —

Just after dark, a light became visible in the far distance, and as the thump, thump, thump of the engines drove the boat forever onwards, other lights appeared until, just before ten o'clock, we found the giant Rock of Gibraltar towering up beside us.

Numerous signal lamps on all sides flashed out their mysterious messages, and we could but wonder what they all meant. At any rate, here was land and, all around us in the darkness, other human beings playing their part in the great game, a thought which seemed to give us a temporary sense of security. However, we soon passed on our way again and, as the last light disappeared on the backward horizon, my pal and I nestled down in our blankets on deck and were soon fast asleep.

Here I should mention that after the first two nights on board, the stuffy atmosphere and the scarcity of space below deck led us to believe that we should find more comfort on deck, and we did. Each morning, however, soon after dawn, members of the ship's crew got busy with hosepipes and swabs, giving the decks a thorough washdown. One night we made our bed at the foot of the stairs leading up to the officers' deck, only to awake early next morning to find water pouring down these stairs and converting our deck into a lake, with our bed creating a miniature island. Without stopping to dress, we snatched up our blankets and ran.

— November 22nd —

Another parade before the MO took place this morning, and this time a dose of vaccine was injected into our arms. As a result, many of the boys, who by this time were almost recovered from seasickness, became invalids again as the result of the vaccination. My dose had very little effect and I was able to carry on as usual, and could generally be found well to the fore in the canteen queue at each opening time.

— November 23rd —

During the day, we sailed into the beautiful Valetta Harbour at Malta, and here gained a first glimpse of people and scenes oriental, although unfortunately we were not allowed to go ashore. The casting of the anchors seemed to be the signal for dozens of Maltese traders to pilot their craft laden with cigarettes, oranges, Turkish Delight etc. from the quay across to us. Then followed a perfect hullaballoo; each merchant trying to oust his rivals by loudly proclaiming the quality and variety of his wares, bargaining with a khaki-clad figure high up on our boat. After much gesticulating on both sides, the enterprising merchant would throw up to his prospective clients a heavy piece of wood or a stone to which was attached one end of a long cord, the other end being tied to a small basket. In this way the customer would draw up the basket and, after placing his money therein, lower it to the merchant. The latter would then count the cash at least three times before delivering the goods, and in the majority of cases the purchaser had good cause to admit that the Maltese were indeed shrewd businessmen.

Perhaps a police boat would now hover in sight, whereat all the traders would pull away as quickly as possible – no doubt their conscience smote them – but as soon as the police had disappeared, back they would come in full force.

In spite of their crude and rather ancient customs, their natural object was to make money, and they knew how to do it. So the British Tommy, always regarded by foreigners as a little millionaire, formed a fine trading centre through which these merchants considerably increased the capitals of their various businesses.

Within a few hours of our arrival, large barges laden with coal, on the top of which squatted gangs of partially clad Maltese labourers, were tugged across to the side of our boat and gangways laid across. Baskets were filled with coal from the barges and carried one by one by the native workmen and emptied into the stoke hold of our boat. As the endless procession proceeded, a solemn dirgeful tune was chanted by the black coal heavers and, as one barge was emptied, so another was brought into position. This went on unceasingly for twenty-four hours, till on the 24th we were ready to continue our journey.

Very soon all signs of land disappeared and once again we were left alone on that apparently illimitable circle of water, the horizon forming a perfect circumference. Occasionally a boat could be seen in the distance – a truly welcome sight – but for the most part our eyes rested on nothing but water.

November 25th

The MO was evidently finding life monotonous again and required some form of entertainment to cheer him up. We were detailed to pay him another visit, when each man was presented with a souvenir in the form of another squirt from his inoculating syringe. As we had already been twice vaccinated before leaving England, we began to think that, if the war lasted many years, we should somewhat resemble a sponge or a pepper-box lid on our return to civilian life.

Nevertheless, one of the Army's strictest disciplinary orders is to obey all orders at once and, if necessary, complain afterwards, so we held out our arms and accepted the perforations like good soldiers, knowing full well that to complain afterwards would be of little avail.

November 27th

At dawn, we found ourselves quite close to land, with the boat steaming round in large circles just outside a large harbour. We learnt this was Moudros, though no one of us was aware (officially) of our ultimate destination, with

Gallipoli, Egypt, Salonika and Mesopotamia each being mentioned by someone 'who knew something'. An hour or so later, however, we entered the harbour, steaming past a truly wonderful array of battleships, hospital ships and submarines of almost all the allies, and finally anchored a mile or so from shore.

There appeared to be no sign of our disembarking, but as the island had the appearance of being a real barren and desolate place, I think the majority of us were pleased to remain aboard. During the past few days the weather had been beautiful and was causing us to surmise that we had entered the zone of semi-tropical weather. Unfortunately we were soon disillusioned, for next morning the weather turned bitterly cold, and before long snow was actually falling.

During the day a party of officers, including our own, went ashore, which fact gave rise to further rumours, but next day the object of their visit was made quite plain when we were ordered to parade with our pay-books. Each private was paid 10*s* and NCO's in proportion. Later in the day various units were transferred to small steamers bound for Suvla and Cape Helles, which lay but a few miles off.

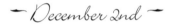

— December 2nd —

This morning we had to parade with rifles and in full kit, before we were transferred across a gangway straight on board a boat called the *Novian*, a horse transport. Here the accommodation for troops was very poor and strictly limited, with the result that we were allotted quarters which had previously been used for stabling horses.

Towards evening, horses were loaded onto the boat and I don't think many of us altogether fancied our present prospects. Fortunately, our stay in these surroundings was very brief for, on the following morning, we were ordered to parade again with full kit and then marched in single file down a gangway on to a small tug called the *Hendon*.

This tug conveyed us across the harbour to an old battleship, the *Magnificent*, which was being used as a transport ship.

What a contrast this presented to the *Novian*! Everywhere and everything aboard was spotless and the very bearing of the boat seemed to spell thoroughness and discipline. As soon as we got aboard, volunteers for stoking were called for but, as the requisite number of men was not forthcoming, conscriptive methods were employed. Next, volunteers were required for the baker's shop, but I was not going to rush into anything of that description, as I knew it would soon be quite hot enough up on deck, let alone the baker's oven!

However, when the requisite number of men had been obtained, the remainder of us were divided up into small parties and detailed permanent guard on various parts of the boat. This, at any rate, was better than coal heaving or getting mixed up with the dough in the baker's shop.

During the afternoon we sailed out of the harbour, the crews of the various battleships and submarines giving us a hearty cheer as we steamed past them. Before sunset we were out of sight of land again and so commenced to make a tour of our new surroundings. Our guard was allotted sleeping quarters right in the forecastle head, with certain members of the crew. To reach these quarters it was necessary to crawl through a kind of trapdoor from the deck, and then climb down a rather steep ladder standing vertically, but we soon overcame the difficulties which we first experienced in reaching our onboard 'home'.

As there were quite a number of men on this guard, the reliefs worked out at two hours on duty and then six hours off, which gave us quite a lot of spare time. On this boat, instead of the usual army breakfast, we were served with hot tea and bread and then given fourpence a day to purchase whatever else we required from the canteen. Of course, everything at the canteen was very cheap and if two or three men put their money together, a real good meal could be obtained.

We had, by this time, passed into (more or less) perpetually sunny latitudes. By lounging about on deck during the day and attending concerts which were held on the officers' deck almost nightly, the time was passing very pleasantly and we were thoroughly enjoying the trip.

— December 6th —

This leisurely way to pass the time continued up until this day, when land became faintly visible on the forward horizon. Everyone was now on the tip-toe of excitement, for surely this was to be the end of our three-week voyage.

In the evening we sailed into the magnificent harbour of Alexandria – this truly seemed a different world to our own, as the setting sun lightly tinted the stately white buildings and gold-capped minarets as they reared their heads above the drooping palms whose branches, gently stirred by the breeze, appeared to be waving us a welcome. All this seemed to immediately convey a sense of ancient mystery and, at the same time, to command a full measure of reverence.

As we moved to our moorings, numerous figures clad in the ancient garb came along the quay, and before the boat was made fast were shouting 'Baksheesh Johnny', as if expressing their only aim in life. And no wonder, for we very soon learnt that their earnest cry translated into English was, 'Give me something for nothing Johnny!'

Having gained a glimpse of this ancient and at once fascinating land, we were all most anxious to set foot ashore and explore its surely wonderful interior.

However, we learnt that we were to remain aboard that night but, in all probability, would land the following morning. The last dwindling rays of sunlight appeared to have left the whole land wrapped in a calm and peaceful atmosphere, making it all the more difficult to realise that our mission was to break this peaceful atmosphere with the rude and ruthless murmurs of war.

That, however, was but a fleeting thought, for the routine of military training which we had undergone was hardly conducive to such sentimental thoughts and reveries, and after silent pondering as to what this new but ancient world held in store for us, I think we all fell asleep with the spirit of adventure strong within us.

— December 7th —

On waking this morning, we were at once conscious of a distinct movement among the troops on board. After breakfast we were ordered to parade on deck with all our kit, and after the usual routine of roll call etc. we proceeded in single file, kitbag on shoulder, down the gangway onto the quay, and for the first time for three weeks set foot once again on terra firma.

During the night a long train had drawn up alongside the quay, and we were soon marshalled onto this.

Here it would perhaps be advisable to point out that the railway coaches on the Egyptian State railways are very different to those in vogue on the British railways. Each coach consists of one long compartment with a door at either end. This door opens from a small platform, which, in order to reach, it is necessary to mount four or five steps from the ground. The interior is arranged after the style of the coaches on some of the London Underground trains; that is, with a gangway down the centre of the entire coach, with the seats arranged on either side of the gangway, each seat capable of holding two persons. There are no glass windows in these coaches but, at regular intervals down each side, there are apertures of about the same size as the ordinary carriage windows. These are fitted with a kind of close fitting venetian blind which can be drawn up or down at will, either to keep out the sun and sand, or to admit light and ventilation.

Each of us having secured a seat and divested ourselves of all equipment which was now lying strewn under the seats, or hung on any hook or nail which presented itself, we were all most anxious for the train to start, Cairo being whispered as our intended objective.

Several hours passed without there being any sign of starting and we were getting somewhat restless. The Army would hardly have felt flattered at the remarks which were passed during that apparently unnecessary delay. However, during our journey from Tidworth, we had already realised that these unaccountable delays were not at all infrequent in military transportation.

At last there was a cry of 'All aboard', and the train moved slowly from the quayside. Gradually gaining speed, we passed stately white buildings in suburban Alexandria, till at last we drew out into flat, open country, where occasional solitary yet stately date palms stood out like sentinels. There were no hedges or woodland here to break the monotony of this wide expanse of flat country. Numerous small ditches, fed from wells of very crude formation, gave an idea of the quaint mode of irrigation which these sons of the Pharaohs still adopted. For a moment, one caught sight of a dark-skinned bearded man, clad in the old robes of biblical history, guiding a wooden plough which was drawn by a camel or perhaps a couple of oxen. A little further on, a colony of camels, goats, fowls and dogs clustered round an assembly of mud hovels all huddled up together, which denoted the manner in which the native elements of the country still existed.

A moment or two later, a dusky maid of the East could be seen adroitly balancing a pitcher of water on her head and walking leisurely towards one of the above mentioned clusters of mud huts. Then a camel bearing an overload of brushwood or sugar-cane and followed by an old native, perched on the very hindmost quarters of a diminutive donkey, would come into sight.

This and numerous other strange sights compelled our attention for a considerable time, but presently a soldier's appetite brought us back to a sense of our real position. Consequently all thoughts of camels, dusky maids and the like were lost in a full realisation of bully beef, apricot jam etc. It would be almost impossible to remember all the strange and interesting sights which met our gaze as we sped onwards, and it would take the pen of a greater writer than me to adequately describe what one could remember. Consequently let us pass on to the time when the train pulled up late that night in Cairo.

3

CAIRO

On passing out of the station into the streets, we were quite dazzled by the street and shop illuminations, and our illusions of an uncivilised country were rudely shattered by the sight of an electric tram coming along the street. A score of Arabs clustered round us, offering for sale a widely varied array of articles ranging from picture postcards to peanuts and cakes. Although to us their language was quite incomprehensible, their facial expressions somewhat enlightened us as to the eagerness and earnestness which their profession demanded. However, we had little time to study closely these interesting characters, for we were soon packed into a tram which bore us, first of all, through busy, noisy streets. Presently however, the lighted thoroughfares were left behind and only an occasional light broke the inky darkness.

At last the tram pulled up and we alighted one by one. We were each amazed to find that our feet sank deep into dry, soft sand. A cool breeze, which seemed to breathe of the desert, greeted us and, as our eyes became accustomed to the darkness, we were able to pick out the dim outline of two huge masses standing on a higher strip of land. Although appearing as mere shadows, their outline was unmistakeable; it was the Pyramids.

It was with a feeling of awe mingled with pride that we realised our close proximity to these wonderful symbols of man's perseverance and determination. We were not allowed long to ponder on that subject however, and within a few minutes we were trudging ankle-deep through fine, soft sand.

Presently a number of small lights became visible which, as we drew nearer, proved to be the lights in the tents of a very large camp. As we halted in the tent lines, a number of men clad only in shorts and shirts emerged from the tents. In the dim candle glow we recognised many of our old pals who had left Tidworth about a month before us. The hour was late, something like two o'clock in the morning, but we were marched to a large marquee and provided with supper. We were then split up into two parties, each party being housed in a large tent. It did not take many minutes to get into our blankets and so to sleep and, I might add, that we readily appreciated the soft sand for a bed after the hard deck of the battleship.

⁓ *December 8th* ⁓

Early this morning, before we had been in bed many hours in fact, we were awakened by the sound of reveille, but as nobody seemed inclined to move (not even the sergeant), we all slept on. A little later however, the sound of fires crackling and the irresistible smell of fried bacon proved mightier than the trumpeter's reveille, and we soon rolled out our blankets and hurriedly performed our ablutions.

We were all agreeably surprised at the breakfast that was provided; plenty of tea, porridge, bacon and bread, causing us to look back with contempt on the chunk of bread decorated with a morsel of tinned salmon which had too often aggravated our appetites at Tidworth. It was well worth crossing an ocean, and even existing for several days on an empty and unruly stomach, to get such a meal as this.

As we sat in the open air, eagerly devouring our rations, the Pyramids looked down on us, no doubt in the same manner in which they had looked down on the camps of soldiers thousands of years before us.

We could now see how this tremendous camp was arranged. The men's quarters, indicated by a myriad of bell tents with a large marquee placed here and there, were situated on a gradual slope. The horse lines were situated on the level ground at the bottom, and beyond these, bordering the road which ran into Cairo, was a huge ration and forage dump. The camp itself was pitched on dry, loose sand, but beyond the road – about three-quarters of a mile away – occasional date palms reared their heads from the midst of cultivated ground.

Soon after breakfast we were paraded and marched to the orderly room where we were very soon introduced to the colonel, adjutant and regimental sergeant major and other notabilities. Now came the somewhat painful moment when our little party had to be broken up, for we were detailed off to various squadrons and troops, there being four troops to a squadron and three squadrons to a regiment. Fortunately, three of us were sent to the same troop. Our names were duly entered on the troop sergeant's roll and he marched us off to the horse lines.

By this time, the sun was getting really hot, making our short march across the hot, soft sand anything but pleasant. On reaching the horse lines, the sight of half-naked perspiring troops busily grooming horses in the excessive heat gave us a slight indication of what lay before us. In that moment, most of us thought almost kindly of Tidworth, at any rate with a feeling more closely allied to kindness than we had ever entertained before.

Having been formally presented to the troop officer who surveyed us with the eye of a cattle dealer, and apparently required our whole pedigree, we were very soon busy with a body brush and curry comb like the rest.

These troop horses, intelligent but oft-times irritating creatures, seemed to know that we were raw recruits to active service; add to this the fact that they were ever the sport of swarms of flies – evidently a relic of one of the ancient plagues of Egypt – and you will to some extent realise how pleasant was our introduction to life 'On Active Service'.

At last, however, a neigh from the horses and a sharp command from the squadron sergeant major denoted that it was time to 'feed up'. As soon as the horses were fed we had to fall in, before being dismissed. Needless to say, we were all soon trudging back across that scorching strip of sand which lay between the horse lines and the tent lines. This time, the general route lay via the canteen, where it was possible to purchase oranges, dates, figs, nuts, tea, cocoa, lemonade and numerous other commodities so well known to the troops on active service.

Soon after reaching our tents, the information came round that it was pontoon for dinner. Now, to us new arrivals, pontoon denoted nothing more than a game of cards which was played a great deal by men with an inclination for speculation. However, the arrival of the very dish in question revealed the fact that it was nothing worse than that very prevalent dish, 'army stew'. Nevertheless, pontoon was a very appropriate name for it, as it was indeed a matter of speculation.

Immediately after dinner there was a rifle inspection. Now, I had only cleaned a rifle about twice before leaving England; consequently I was getting the wind up somewhat as, minute by minute, the ordeal grew closer. At last, at the dreaded 'Fall in C. Squadron' command, my heart seemed to fall into my boots.

There we stood on parade, four troops of khaki-clad figures, alert and with sun helmets set at various angles of rakishness, and every now and then a mocking flash of sunlight was reflected from the bolt or nuzzle of a rifle whose owner had used something more than the regulation oil and dry rag which was laid down in the army book of instruction.

'Shun!' The four troop officers appeared simultaneously. Oh wretched sand that would so persistently get into one's boots, why would it not cover me altogether?

'For inspection, port arms.' The seconds seemed like hours as the officer, examining each rifle in turn, got gradually nearer. After a few rapid movements with the bolt of my rifle and the usual examination of the magazine, I was conscious of a withering glance from the eye of the 'one pipper' as he triumphantly held up an oil-tipped finger, indicating the presence of oil in the magazine of my rifle. At any rate he passed on to the head of the line.

Then came the order, 'Examine arms.'

On this command each man had to bring his rifle into such a position that the officer could look down the barrel. Again, as the officer approached, I was conscious of a distinct quivering at the knees and, at last, the storm broke. After a rapid glance down the barrel of my rifle, the officer in a tone of sarcastic alarm called out, 'Sergeant! Just look at this man's rifle. It's a perfect disgrace to the British Army; not only dirty but rusty. Rusty!'

With an air of woefulness, mingled with fear, the sergeant glanced at my rifle, and at me, and acquiesced; of course he did, that was his duty. Turning again to me, with now a greater proportion of sarcasm in his utterings, the officer continued, 'I thought they made soldiers at Tidworth; what do you mean by coming on parade with a rifle in that disgraceful state?'

Murmuring something to the effect that the rifle was rusty when issued to me, I was cut short by being ordered to go and clean it again and present it to the troop sergeant for inspection in an hour's time. So, during the next hour while everybody else lounged, or lolled, half-naked in the tents, I sweated away most conscientiously polishing every part of my rifle which, ultimately, was passed by the sergeant as being satisfactory.

Scarcely had I finished this job when stable call was sounded and we had to water and feed the horses. This was half an hour's work, and the dismissal from that parade ended the day's work unless, of course, one was detailed for night guard.

It was now about half past four in the afternoon. As at breakfast and dinner, the food provided for tea was excellent. This excellence of food, we ascertained, was made possible by a grant from the Egyptian Government.

The sun was now gradually approaching the horizon and, as its last brilliant rays disappeared, darkness and a cool, damp atmosphere crept over the scene. A myriad of lights sprang up all over the camp, giving the whole scene the appearance of what one imagines as fairyland.

In company with several other men from the regiment, I paid a visit to the canteens which were all run by natives and here, amidst the fevered excitement of Crown and Anchor etc., many an eagerly awaited 'letter from the front' was pieced together. Over a cup of native-brewed tea and some sickly native-made cakes, we sat and reviewed our present position, and while feeling that we were a very long way from home, agreed unanimously that it was better than being at Tidworth.

Quite early we returned to our tents and, one by one, put down our blankets and settled down for the night.

Before we got to sleep, however, various members of the squadron who had been on pass to Cairo returned with wonderful stories of its glamour, making us all long to see the place for ourselves. As we remained in this camp for just over a month, it is unnecessary to give a detailed account of each day's happenings, but instead give a general idea of what took place …

The routine was on somewhat similar lines to that at Tidworth, only that the horses being stabled out in the open necessitated rather different arrangements here. Then the climate had to be taken into consideration also. Reveille was earlier than in England, and during the hottest part of the day it was physically impossible to work at all strenuously.

Each morning the horses were exercised and groomed. In the afternoon we spent an hour on saddle or manual instruction, or something of that description.

Every day a certain number of passes to Cairo were issued which permitted the holder to be absent from camp from two o'clock till eleven o'clock. These passes were issued by strict rotation so that everyone had a turn about once a week.

As the days passed by, we gradually became more accustomed to the climate and the general routine and, on the whole, in spite of night guards, day guards, fatigues etc., the days passed fairly pleasantly.

The climate made it difficult to realise that Christmas was just a few weeks ahead. It was freely rumoured that the festive day was to be celebrated right royally, and that the mess huts, which were now nearing completion, were to be ready and officially opened on Christmas Day.

During our first few days here, those – and they were few – who had any money, gradually converted it into Egyptian Piasters; 1 piaster being worth 2½d. We quickly realised that, to obtain the fullest value, half-crowns were the best coins to convert as they would realise 12 piasters, whereas a florin fetched, in most cases, only 9 piasters, which of course was only 1/10½d. From this it will be observed that we had very quickly put into practice the old sergeant major's advice concerning 'number one first'. It was essential too, for the natives were real hot stuff on exchanges. Indeed, it seemed that in every bit of khaki they saw a chance to get rich quick.

※

My active service career was but a few days old when I was rapidly brought into prominence, but the manner in which it happened left me feeling that I had far better have remained in obscurity.

It happened one morning when we were exercising the horses. Each man present rode one horse and led two others. The particular horse I was riding suddenly reared up and then rolled over with me. I picked myself up and remounted, but the action was repeated and my two led horses, surprised at their unexpected liberty, were soon galloping gaily round the camp.

An officer eventually caught the runaways, and so for the third time I mounted.

All went well for a minute or two, and then the brute I was riding suddenly seized the bit between its teeth and bolted with me. My first impulse was to try and jump clear and leave this wild creature to continue its meteoric career as it thought fit. On second thoughts, however, I determined to stick to it, and consequently put every ounce of strength I possessed into pulling on the reins. In one mad whirl we rushed past tent lines, horse lines and water troughs, and rapidly approached the forage dump where huge stacks of corn etc. presented a rather formidable obstacle should this steed endeavour to jump them. At last, standing up in the stirrups and reaching as far forward as possible, I gave one final jerk on the reins and, with a mighty sigh, the beggar came to a dead stop, incidentally giving me a very intimate view of its ears.

Rapidly dismounting, I found both the horse and myself wet through with perspiration. Whispering a few curt but most expressive words into the ear of my rather too gallant a charge, I led him back to the horse lines. Here I was naturally greeted with many rude and sarcastic remarks and was ordered to walk my horse about until it cooled down sufficiently to be watered. Perhaps it is hardly necessary to add, but I gave that horse a very wide berth in the future.

The days passed quickly by and my turn for a pass into Cairo came at last. During our early days on active service many new friendships sprang up but, speaking generally, most of us found one particular pal. In my case it was a fellow slightly older than me and who, at that time, I knew very little about. Fate had thrown us together on the latter part of our journey out from England and, soon after reaching Mena, we found ourselves together on night guard in the damp, chilly desert air, which was enough to cement friendship. And so it came about that we started out together on our first trip into Cairo.

A walk of half a mile or so brought us to the tram terminus where we had alighted on the night of our arrival from England. We boarded a tram and, after a ride of twenty minutes or so, crossed one of the many beautiful bridges which span the Nile and Cairo lay at our feet.

Everything appeared entrancing and, as we alighted it was with a feeling of great confusion, not knowing which way to look first. The wide and well-kept thoroughfares were thronged with natives garbed in robes of every imaginable hue; Europeans in white or khaki drill suits and large pith helmets; Arab boys darting about in all directions, some of them offering for sale wares of some description or other, and others merely asking for 'baksheesh'. A general air of drowsiness pervaded the whole place; no one – except the Arab boys – appeared to be in a hurry, or to have anything particular to do.

For a time, we wandered about aimlessly like the rest of the population, meeting with something to arrest our attention at every step; first a particularly fine shop, then a camel laden with sugar cane, striding with ungainly gait along the street followed by a group of Arab boys who, at every possible opportunity, would sneak a length of sugar cane; the famous Shepheards Hotel, Ezbekieh Gardens and other objects of interest claimed our attention for some considerable time.

In spite of our wonderful Eastern surroundings, however, we were still English and, like true Englishmen, by this time were hungry and thirsty. Consequently, in the welcome shade and seclusion of a quiet little café, a very comfortable hour was spent over a very dainty and thoroughly European meal.

By the time we entered the streets again, the sun was well on its downward course, throwing its lengthening beams onto the impressive white buildings and transforming domes and minarets into palaces of gold, and revealing, even to us, the 'romance and glamour' of the East we thought to be merely a stock description emanating from the novelist's glib pen.

It would perhaps be as well to point out that we were seeing Cairo through the eyes of British Tommies, enjoying a few hours of liberty with the future an unknown quantity, and endeavouring to abstract the maximum enjoyment in a minimum time. Consequently, many things which would undoubtedly have left an indelible impression on the mind of the tourist or traveller passed almost unnoticed by us.

It was not surprising then, that after a further short stroll round the principal streets, we soon found ourselves seated at a table of one of the numerous cafés – drinking houses – which could be found at almost every step throughout the city. A waiter came and took our order and, on a small platform at one end of the room, a band enlivened the proceedings with a series of local 'masterpieces'.

British and Australian Tommies and natives of all classes rubbed shoulders in this unfamiliar corner of the globe. As we sat there, we were continually pestered by street Arabs trying to sell us picture postcards, cigarettes, cakes, peanuts and a hundred and one other things, till, becoming fed up with them and having already picked up a few Arab words (not by any means the choicest), we politely told them to 'imshee!' (hop it).

At nine o'clock, time was called for the troops and so, after a final short stroll along the streets, we were glad to get a tram back to camp, hardly realising that those few very pleasant hours in Cairo had been other than a dream.

❦

Two days which were red-letter days in our existence, and which came round all too infrequently, were pay day and mail day. The former came round each alternate Friday, but the latter? Heaven knew when. However, a few days before Christmas, we received our first active service mail bringing the first tidings of the land which we had left seven weeks before. Needless to say, it was a day of great rejoicings.

The next great day was Christmas Day, which we had all been looking forward to. Routine was to be the same as a normal Sunday, with church parade in the morning followed by just the necessary stable duties. At the usual dinner hour it had been arranged that we were to have a real Christmas dinner, with turkey, plum pudding and all the trimmings. Unfortunately, the catering arrangements had been placed in the hands of a local firm of caterers, with the result that the 'spread' was a fiasco for us, but no doubt very satisfactory from the caterer's point of view. The good things were provided alright, but in such small quantities that most of us retired from the feast considerably hungrier than when we sat down, and were jolly glad to tighten up our belts with a few added trifles from the canteen – that was our 'Merry Christmas'.

4

SALHIEH

Shortly after Christmas, rumours of a pending move were in circulation and, when we commenced parades with full equipment and packed saddles, we knew there was something afoot. The murmurs increased daily, both in quantity and degree, till at last, on January 4th, we received marching orders.

We paraded at eleven o'clock that night in full marching order and, after much excitement with nervous horses etc., we eventuality started off for Cairo about an hour and a half later.

Arriving at the station somewhere in the early hours of the morning, it took some considerable time to get the horses aboard the train, after which we found seats for ourselves. Most of us were properly tired out and fast asleep before the train actually started, and very soundly we must have slept too, for, when I woke up, the sun was well on its way across the heavens and the only view through the carriage window was one of sand and palm trees. No one appeared to know exactly where we were and there was nothing in sight to help us at all.

Not long after, however, the train drew up and, on receiving the order to alight, found we were at a small wayside station in the desert whose name was proudly displayed in large bold letters – 'Salhieh' – but of course that conveyed practically nothing to us.

After unloading the horses and baggage, we saddled up, mounted and then crossed the railway line to find that, beyond a small collection of mud hovels on the fringe of the palm grove, there was nothing but miles of bare desert.

It was on this open ground, just outside the village, that we pitched our camp.

This was our first experience of pitching camp, and a long and dreary job it seemed, especially as a mild sandstorm sprang up long before we had finished. At any rate, by teatime the horse lines had been laid down (that was the first job of all), the horses themselves watered, groomed and fed, and then our own tents unpacked and erected in perfectly straight lines and at equal distances apart.

At first we were not particularly enamoured with this place called Salhieh as, apart from a troop of Royal Engineers, we were the only troops in the place, and consequently things were pretty dull. Later on, however, we always looked back on our sojourn at Salhieh as the happiest period of our whole army career.

Instead of being officially an army of occupation, we now became an expeditionary force, and consequently there was a general tightening up of routine and especially discipline. Mounted parades and tactical schemes took the place of exercise, and on each mounted parade an inspection was made to see that horses were properly groomed, and that saddles, boots, and all equipment had been thoroughly cleaned.

Nevertheless, our leisure hours, if rather few, were very happy, and a healthy state of camaraderie soon developed amongst all the men of the regiment.

When we became an expeditionary force, the ration allowance which we had enjoyed from the Egyptian Government ceased, and consequently we soon began to look out for other means by which to supplement the ordinary army rations.

In the village, eggs were plentiful and cheap, and at all times of the day it was possible to buy these, either hard-boiled or raw, from the natives who soon became aware of the fact that 'plenty business' was to be done in and around the camp.

Other ways of adding to the variety of our menu were perhaps not quite so legitimate, but nevertheless were exploited to the full. For instance, on the borders of the village we discovered several melon beds and orange plantations which, under cover of darkness, received our due attention.

One dark night, several of us set out to raid a certain plantation of which we had taken note during the day. After successfully negotiating numerous ditches and making our way through prickly cactus hedges, we hurriedly filled a nosebag with fruit, incidentally being chased by several natives and their dogs. Imagine our disgust when we got back to camp and found the bag was full of lemons and citrons!

During our leisure hours, we were permitted to go into the village which consisted of a kind of market square adjoining the railway station, from which, on the opposite end of the line, ran the main narrow street, which was lined on either side with pokey one-storey shops. In each shop squatted the proprietor, surrounded on all sides by his various wares.

This village of Salhieh was situated in the fertile region of what was, in biblical days, the land of Goshen, and it was through this very country that the Israelites passed on their way to the Red Sea.

Although poor and in a low state of civilisation, it was immediately noticeable how devoutly religious the whole population was; at least there was a very outward sign of this, for it was a common sight to see a man wash his feet and hands in the little brook which flowed through the village and then, facing east, fall down on his knees and pray.

During our stay here I was unfortunate enough to be plagued with boils, which earned me a week or two of light duty. As light duty was a name which embraced endless duties, I began to think that hard labour would have been a lighter task. Before long, however, I was on full duty again.

As in the camp at Mena, so in the early days here meals were served in the open, each man drawing his food in his mess tin and consuming it in the tent. Early in February, a gang of native carpenters arrived on the scene and commenced to erect a number of mess huts. At Mena, no sooner were the mess huts ready for use than we received orders to move. Consequently there was now much jesting concerning the new huts in course of construction. The native workmen appeared to work so leisurely that it looked as if we would remain here for some months, even if we again received marching orders as soon as the huts were complete.

Strangely enough, that is what did happen. Various rumours had been in circulation and everything in our routine and training had pointed to a move towards the fighting zone. Definite orders were issued early in March.

— March 16th —

On this morning our saddles were packed, tents struck and all baggage and stores conveyed to the railway station ready to move off the following day.

As usual, a small party of men was detailed to travel by train with the baggage and, on account of my recent attack of boils, it included me.

5

BALLAH AND BALLY BUNION

This morning we moved off. For some miles the railway carried us through palm groves and fertile areas till we came to the sand banks of the Suez Canal. Here we branched off to the right and ran parallel with the canal on the Port Said–Port Suez Line, which runs for the whole distance by the side of the canal. However, we did not get far along the canal, just a matter of a few miles to a small desert station called Ballah.

Before we arrived, a sandstorm of considerable violence had sprung up, and did its best to choke and blind us during the unloading operations. It was some hours later, as night was falling, when our regimental transport arrived to pick up the baggage, and we then learnt that camp was being pitched just over a mile away.

By the time we arrived, the tents had been erected and everybody was already settling down. Life in this place opened with a liveliness which forecast a somewhat busy future. On the day of our arrival, one squadron was sent out immediately to cross the canal at Khantara and proceed to (as far as we could ascertain) a place called Duiedar – an oasis of some considerable size which lay some miles east of the canal. At the same time, one troop from our own squadron moved across the canal from Ballah to a place called Bally Bunion, which was a mere contour on the map some four or five miles east of the canal. (At both Khantara and Ballah there was a pontoon bridge across the Suez.)

For the next fortnight or so, the remainder of the squadron were kept busy with troop drill and squadron drill intermingled with numerous fatigue duties. One bright feature of our life here was that we were permitted to bathe in the canal each afternoon. This meant a fairly long walk, of course, but a dip in the cool salt water made the pilgrimage well worthwhile.

For a time I was unable, through force of circumstances, to take much active interest in anything but the daily sick parade with its consequent visit to the medical lines. The fact of the matter was that I was again the victim of one of Egypt's own particular plagues – boils – which attacked me in such manner that I found it considerably easier to stand than sit down. However, after several very intimate encounters with the doctor's venomous little knife and plenty of salt-water bathing, I was at length able to renew acquaintances with my horse and saddle.

— April 17th —

This morning, our troop (thirty of us), in the charge of the troop officer, formed up according to orders in full marching kit and moved off across the canal to relieve the troop at Bally Bunion.

Once across the pontoon bridge we found ourselves in real desert country, the only signs of vegetation being an occasional tuft of camel weed. There was, however, a light railway track running straight ahead, and this we followed for some four or five miles till we came upon a small cluster of bell tents nestled snugly in a shallow depression of the ground. This was Bally Bunion, the terminus of the light railway.

It was with light hearts and a feeling of great satisfaction that we dismounted, for we were now free from the usual red tape methods which were always very much in evidence when the whole regiment was camped together under the very nose of the colonel.

We soon learnt that our duties here would be to form, daily, two outposts some three or four miles in front of the camp, and to patrol alternately to two hods (palm groves or oases), some six or seven miles further ahead. Both of these hods were a well of water, and any advancing hostile troops would naturally make for these points.

This barren country presented very few distinctive landmarks, and early morning mists were the rule rather than the exception. For direction, it was necessary to rely almost solely on the compass, though certain lectures which we had received enabled us to use the sun and, at night, the stars — a very useful medium for that purpose.

— April 18th —

As dawn was breaking, we rode out of camp — an officer, two NCOs and twelve other ranks to peep into the vast desert. Our first objective was a high sand ridge, very like the rest of the country to our unaccustomed eyes, from the summit of which the country around lay open to view for many miles.

Several men, including two signallers, were posted here. Away to the right front, a mile or so distant, another ridge rose up rather higher than those around it. This was our next objective, and here another small party was posted. The remainder of the party proceeded still further to patrol as far as one of the hods previously mentioned.

Through wild sandy country and among many high ridges, the patrol threaded its way carefully and cautiously, with an ever-watchful eye for footprints or hoof prints in the sand, or for the outline of any suspicious object silhouetted on the skyline.

The sun was scorching hot and its glare so intense that it caused even the smallest object to cast a jet black shadow of its own form on the almost-white sand. A deep silence and stillness enveloped us, the only sign of movement being the occasional rising of a large bird as it was disturbed by our approach.

At intervals we came across the sun-bleached bones of a camel long since dead, or the evil-smelling carcase of one more recently deceased, and on which the carrion birds now fed.

Towards midday we approached a very high sand ridge running across our front. At the foot of this ridge we dismounted, and two of us were ordered to crawl to the summit and see what lay on the other side. Never shall I forget the sight which met our eyes as we peeped over. The ridge itself was of some considerable length and sloped down on the far side at an amazingly steep angle for several hundred feet. For miles around lay a vast area of fairly flat, barren country, but tucked away at the foot of the ridge appeared a tiny cluster of date palms whose green leaves, in the midst of that scorching desert, were the most refreshing sight I had ever seen. It almost appeared that a small crumb of England had been inadvertently dropped there by an unseen hand. Looking farther afield, beyond the palms, we could see a number of Bedouin shacks built of dried palm branches but, as there was no sign of life, we concluded the erstwhile inhabitants had departed.

After two men had been posted at the top of this ridge, the remainder of the party descended, by a narrow winding track, down to the hod below. It was a fairly easy matter to find the well of water which we knew to exist here, it being merely a hole in the ground with its mouth propped open by means of palm trunks. The water was too brackish for us to drink, at least while we had fresh water in our bottles, but the horses were very glad of a good fill, after which they were quite ready for the feed which we carried on our saddles. And soon enough we were also lolling comfortably in the shadow of the palms, making short work of our own rations.

After an hour or so of rest we started on the return journey which, in my case, became a very painful matter long before it was over (because of my boils). Consequently, the last few miles of the ride were somewhat in the nature of torture to me, and it will be readily imagined what relief there was when we came in sight of first the outposts which we had dropped in the morning and, finally, the camp itself.

On arrival, the stable duties were quickly accomplished, after which we were dismissed to prepare for the hot meal served up to us in the evening – a meal to which our thoughts had oft-times wandered during the ride back to camp. After this meal there was nothing to do but sit in our tents and yarn and sing, except, of course, when it was one's turn for night guard.

Many happy hours were spent in the cool evening air gossiping on various topics, but generally it was Blighty. How eagerly we awaited the mail, for we knew nothing of what was happening beyond our own horizon, and even at that early period of the war, we half expected that each mail would bring news that on the Western Front the end of the war was in sight. A good thing, perhaps, that news was scarce and that by the time it reached us it was old, otherwise I fear we should never have remained such optimists. As it was, our gossiping invariably ended with the consoling resolution that the first ten years would be the worst.

For some little time I was, again, a regular attendant at the tent of the medical officer. Fortunately for me, our own was not with us and our troop officer took me personally to the medical officer of an infantry detachment nearby. Here I received more sympathetic treatment and had to appear three times a day for hot fomentations which, in a comparatively short time, put me right.

About a week after our arrival at Bally Bunion we experienced the worst sandstorm we had encountered so far, and, as it eventually turned out, the worst we ever did encounter.

It was quite dark all day and the ever-moving clouds of sand made it impossible to see many yards ahead. No patrol was able to go out that day, although several attempts were made. Tents were blown down and the shapes of small hills were completely altered in a few hours.

Apart from this solitary storm however, we spent quite a happy time at this place and learnt quite a lot concerning life in the desert.

— April 21st (Good Friday) —

We were relieved by another troop and returned to the regiment at Ballah.

— April 23rd (Easter Sunday) —

We were now settling down again to ordinary camp life and, as a canteen had sprung up during our absence at Bally Bunion, we anticipated enjoying to the fullest extent the many little luxuries which this canteen offered.

On this particular evening as darkness came on, the numerous candles which sprang up all around made it apparent that in practically every tent, quiet revels, made possible by purchases from the canteen, were in progress. The notes of a mouth organ rang out here and there, with singing and laughter coming from almost every tent.

Suddenly the notes of a trumpet were heard above everything else, and in an instant everything was quiet, for we recognised the trumpeter's call; it was the alarm.

Within a moment or two every man was on parade and the order given to pack saddles and be ready to move off at a moment's notice – the Turks were attacking our outposts on the other side of the canal. Gathering up our kit as quickly as possible, there was a general exodus to the horse lines where, by flickering candles, we packed our saddles as best we could.

Having packed our saddles and filled our water bottles, the best thing now was to snatch a wink of sleep. Just as we were getting down to it, the sergeant came round with the news that reveille would be at half two in the morning and we were to move off three-quarters of an hour later. Needless to say, an avalanche of questions were simultaneously hurled at the sergeant who, true to tradition, knew nothing officially apart from the orders he gave to us, although he had heard rumours that our other two squadrons had been cut up by the Turks. With that we rolled up in our blankets and were soon asleep.

Half Past Two in the Morning
A murmur and I feel the cold, damp air of early morning coming in through the tent door. I raise myself and can distinguish other dark forms around me doing likewise, and I hear the last blatant strains of that evil-sounding call, reveille. Never had it been a welcome sound but on this particular occasion it was more repulsive than ever, seeming to boast of its almost tyrannical power.

In a moment or two, a score of candles sprang up on a scene of great activity and bustle. No one was happy, tempers were ruffled but there was no time to waste, for the horses had to be watered and fed before we could have our own breakfast.

There is nothing like activity for regaining equilibrium of temper, and so by the time we had saddled up and were ready to move off, we had fully regained our usual British Tommy equanimity.

Of course it was still dark when we moved off but, by the time we had crossed the pontoon bridge over the canal, the first signs of daybreak were appearing, and by the time we reached Bally Bunion it was broad daylight. Here we merely stayed to water the horses and then moved on over the ground with which we had become so familiar during the past fortnight.

For the greater part of the day we patrolled as far as the hod we had previously visited, but we found no signs of hostile troops and so in the late afternoon we returned to Bally Bunion.

We now learnt that our other two squadrons, who had been operating on our left, had been surprised by the Turks who had got right into their camp at Duiedar. On our particular front everything was quiet but the whole squadron now remained here at Bally Bunion to carry out the daily patrols and outpost duties.

For a whole month we remained here and, on the whole, had quite a good time. During this period, however, we experienced a real heat wave with the shade temperature remaining well over 100°F for several successive days. This finally acclimatised us.

— *May 24th (Empire Day)* —

We once again crossed the canal and returned to Ballah. The next fortnight passed by somewhat uneventfully, most of the time being devoted to various items of training such as mounted drill, tactical schemes etc., not forgetting the numerous guards and fatigues always associated with camp life.

It was while we were on one of these tactical schemes that we witnessed our first mirage. As we rode along over absolute barren country there appeared in the far distance a pool of clear water encircled by palm trees whose forms were reflected in the surface. At first we thought it was something real (and how refreshing it looked) but, as we rode on towards it for some considerable time, we found ourselves no nearer to it and it was only then that we realised that it was a mirage.

6

KHANTARA

The whole brigade moved across the canal at Khantara: a point on the canal several miles north of Ballah. Khantara was the main base on the canal for operations on the Sinai Peninsula. Earlier in the war, the Turks had advanced as far west as this when our main defences were on the west bank of the canal.

From Khantara a full gauge single-line railway ran eastward into the desert for some twenty miles to a place called Romani. There was also a good metal road for some miles running parallel with the railway. A short distance from the canal, on the right of the road, was an aerodrome consisting of one or two hangars housing several almost obsolete planes and a few bell tents.

On the opposite side of the road was a YMCA canteen and by the side of that we pitched our camp. Another small cluster of bell tents, a few marquees, a forage dump on the bank of the canal and that is about all there was of Khantara at that time.

The only means of transport across the canal was by means of the pontoon bridge, which was only wide enough to take traffic passing in one direction at a time. Consequently a military policeman was always on duty at either end of the bridge to regulate the traffic flow. Not long after we had arrived, I was detailed for police duty on the bridge, and for a week or so I proudly wore the initials MP on a red armlet. This was a nice easy job which would have suited me for the duration, but a week was the limit for such a cushy job.

The weather was now so hot that all drills etc. were done in the early morning. During the afternoon we were glad to lie in our tents, almost nude, until four o'clock when we all had to turn out to groom, water and feed the horses.

On Whit Sunday afternoon, however, we were reminded that the Turks were still active, for they sent a messenger in the form of an aeroplane which flew over the camp and dropped quite a few bombs. Fortunately for us, the plane was at too high an altitude to drop its cargo with any great accuracy, and as a result little damage was done.

After spending three or four weeks here at Khantara, our squadron and one other moved forward some four or five miles to a point known as Hill 70. Here we joined the New Zealand Mounted Rifles, who we soon found to be a very fine lot of fellows and the best of pals, which made our association with them of the happiest possible nature.

Hill 70, as the name implies, was a hill – of sand of course – and naturally there was no form of shelter against aerial attack. A camp of cavalry made a good target for an aeroplane as the horse lines stood out in quite bold relief on the almost white sand. Almost every morning at precisely the same time (while we were breakfasting), Turkish planes would come over and pay us a visit. At the first sign of their approach we had to run and untie our horse, mount and ride out of camp as quickly as possible. The idea was to get the horses scattered as much as possible before the bombs fell. This became almost a daily parade and we got quite used to it and, as far as I know, no serious casualties occurred.

One day, early in July, the troop officer sent for me and asked whether I would like a trip to Port Said on the following day to order stores for the officers' mess. Having thanked him profusely for the offer, which I accepted on the spot, he gave me particulars of what I was to do, and a pass and railway warrant to Port Said.

Next morning I caught a train (a goods train of course) down to Khantara where I had to change and cross the pontoon bridge to Khantara West, which was on the Egyptian State Railways. Here I caught a passenger train and, by the middle of the morning, was in Port Said for the first time.

I had plenty of shopping to do but found time to partake of one or two good meals during the course of the day. In the evening, when I boarded the train back to Khantara, I felt that I had just spent the most enjoyable day of my whole army career. A somewhat tedious return journey landed me back in camp somewhere about three o'clock the next morning.

— July 27th (my 21st birthday) —

Our troop and one other set out at five-thirty in the morning to sink wells at a small oasis called Bir-el-Nusse, which lay some four or five miles ahead. On commencing operations we were surprised to find how near the surface water lay and it was not long before we had discarded boots and socks and even breeches as we sank below water level.

Our greatest trouble came from the fact that we were digging in sand, and that the sides kept washing in. It was, therefore, necessary to dig the hole wider than it was deep to begin with, then, as we dug deeper, we worked towards the centre. When the requisite depth had been reached, the sides were propped up with sheets of corrugated zinc held firm with posts of timber wedged from corner to corner at top and bottom.

In two days we constructed two satisfactory wells and then returned to Hill 70. Upon our return, it was apparent that in a very short time we should be moving up further into the desert.

⎯ *August 4th* ⎯

Our expectations were soon fulfilled, for early in the morning we moved off in full marching order, presumably to the next station on the railway line, called Gilban.

Arriving there we off-saddled and were about to put down the horse lines when we suddenly received the order to saddle-up again, draw rations and fill our water bottles from the pipeline which ran up as far as this point.

These duties had to be performed so hurriedly that there was some confusion in issuing rations, and some of us only got a ration of bread without any bully beef or anything else. Before moving off, we were told that no water was to be drunk until the order was given. That sounded as though there was serious business ahead.

Soon we were riding over the scorching hot sands of the desert and continued thus until about midday, when we halted to feed the horses and ourselves. We were now permitted to take a sip of water from our bottles. As previously mentioned, the ration for many of us was a day's ration of bread, but fortunately for me I was able to join in with a chum of mine who had a tin of sausages which he had bought some time previously from the canteen.

Although there was not much time for reflection, it certainly appeared somewhat incongruous that here, in the midst of the Sinai Desert, whose wide expanse had carried the footprints of men whose names had been carried down to us from the times when half the world was undiscovered, that we should be calmly regaling ourselves from a tin whose contents – so the label informed us – had been manufactured in that most modern country, America. This reflection, however, in no way deterred us from enjoying that product of the New World.

We were soon in the saddle again and the sun seemed to get fiercer every minute. The country now began to get more irregular with high sand ridges jutting up in many places, and on the horizon in front of us appeared a range of high hills. As we drew nearer, the sound of rifle and machine gun fire reached us, and an occasional puff of white smoke denoted the bursting of shrapnel shells in the far distance.

At last we reached the foot of these hills and dismounted. Advancing on foot, troop by troop, we could hear the sound of every shot that was fired go echoing through the valleys all round. Before it was our turn to crawl to the top of one of the ridges, we saw many wounded men being brought down; quite a cheerful start!

We were soon crawling up to the top of one of the ridges, and as soon as we peeped over the top and raised our rifles to fire in response to the fire order from our troop officer, a shower of enemy bullets 'pinged' over us and all about us, spitting up little puffs of sand wherever they landed.

Shells were soon coming uncomfortably close to us, most of them bursting in the gulley just behind us, and the first impulse was to imitate the ostrich and bury one's head in the sand, for we all felt that every bullet that came over was specially intended for us. We soon got used to this, however, and one by one we raised our heads, displaying a sand-tipped nose and mouth in some cases, showing how earnest one's intention of keeping low had been. The heat from the sun and, no doubt, the fright of those initial bullets had caused us to sweat rather profusely, with the result that the sand adhered quite firmly to our faces and we laughed at each other.

Before long we were peering over the ridge and carrying out the officer's fire orders with complete contempt for the bullets which pinged and hissed around us. The sound of an approaching shell still caused us to duck, however, with its weird screeching approach and fierce ravaging snarl as it burst, stamping it as a bad investment!

So things went on until it got dark and the firing died down. It was possible to detect shots that were fired by the little tongue of flame which shot out from the muzzle. We were now allowed to take another sip of water and, what with the smoke and powder from the rifles and bursting shells in addition to the heat of the sun – now fortunately sunk – it can perhaps be imagined with what joy and relief the order was received.

The next order was to get back to our horses, which were concealed in one of the gullies behind us, and soon we were riding back across the desert, the moon and stars being the only things visible. As we rode along we learnt of the many casualties that had taken place in the scrap, and many riderless horses formed part of our rather dejected cavalcade.

Until we had ridden some miles, smoking was forbidden – across the desert, even a match light can be seen for miles. When at last permission to smoke was given, the flickering lights which sprang up all along the column testified to the popularity of the order.

So we jaunted along, knee to knee, almost asleep, chilled to the bone and not having the slightest idea where we were going, except that where we were headed had water for both horses and men (by this point, most of us had drunk our last swig).

On and on we rode with just an occasional halt of five minutes to rest the horses until, somewhere between one and two o'clock in the morning, we came to a small camp which we learnt was Pelussium. We watered the horses and filled our bottles, then snatched a few hours' rest.

Early the next morning we started back again in pursuit of the Turks. Arriving at length on the scene of our action of the previous day, we found the Turks had retired, so on we went, riding through almost blue heat, till at about two o'clock in the afternoon we were welcomed by a volley of shrapnel and high explosive shells; the Turks had apparently retired to a rather large palm grove called Katia, which contained several wells of water.

As we were now operating several miles ahead of our own fresh water supplies, it was necessary for us to capture the grove if possible. So we proceeded to the attack, but the very fierce resistance which we met made it evident that the place was strongly held and that the Turks intended to hang onto it.

We, of course, were advancing across open ground but the Turks were well dug in so that a very fierce action went on for some hours until it became apparent that, with our comparatively small numbers, we would have to get out of it.

As we did so, we were heavily shelled and one of our troop officers was killed. Several men were too exhausted to get back to their horses quick enough and fell into the hands of the Turks. Among these were two of my pals from Nuneaton.

Our water had now all gone and there was no telling how long it would be before we got a further supply. However, for the moment we were only too glad to gallop out of action.

For hours we rode back, but now both horses and men were nearly frantic with thirst. After several hours of riding, our thirst became so intense that some of us were glad to suck a tablet which we carried for sterilising brackish water and consequently contained a strong acid. We were far too parched to talk and could hardly sit still in our saddles.

Of course it had been dark for some hours and nobody seemed to know exactly where we were, but at last we came to a cluster of palm trunks and … water.

Then followed a scene of great confusion, in spite of all orders to the contrary: the horses became almost uncontrollable and many of the men too.

The well was small in circumference and the water deep down, so that it all had to be drawn up a bucketful at a time.

When the first bucketful came up, horses and men struggled together to get their lips to it. By degrees we all got a drink and, although the water was horribly brackish, it was to us the purest water that had ever moistened our lips. We drank and drank again, and the horses seemed that they would never have their fill, poor beggars.

It turned out that we were now close to Romani, where we had been in action the previous day. So we rode into Romani where we drew rations and refilled our water bottles with fresh water, and after a quick meal of bully and biscuits were glad to get down to an hour or two's sleep.

At dawn we were up and off again after the Turks. Eventually we came in sight of our battleground of the previous day and found to our great relief that they had again retired.

On we went in pursuit and found them holding the next palm grove called Oghretina. Again a rather fierce shellfire greeted our approach, and again several hours of scrapping took place, till in the late afternoon we withdrew to Katia where there was plenty of well water.

After watering and feeding the horses, rations were issued and we were informed that we were to have several hours' rest. Although it was then nearing midnight, hardly a man got down to sleep before having a wash and, with the aid of a candle, a shave; making it the first wash and shave we had had for four days.

How peaceful were our slumbers that night, rolled up in our blankets on the soft sand, with the moonlight darting through the branches of the palm trees all around.

Next morning, after performing the usual stable duties – grooming, watering and feeding the horses – we were allowed to do pretty well as we pleased. A casual stroll through the grove revealed to some extent the damage we had wrought on the Turks during the fighting of the previous few days. A field dressing station had been formed and our own Royal Army Medical Corps were bringing in wounded Turks from all directions. There they lay on stretchers, a dejected company, some writhing in pain, and though they were our enemies it was impossible to look on them without a feeling of pity and remorse for, like ourselves, they had relatives and friends back home; that was the thought that struck us.

A night's rest, a meal or two and a wash and shave had been like a tonic to us, and so in the late afternoon when the order was issued, 'Saddle-up,' we carried it out quite cheerfully. It was explained to us that we were going out to a small palm grove called Ameysa away on our right flank, to ascertain whether the Turks had retired from there.

In all movements of mounted troops, a screen of six or eight men riding in pairs, the whole forming a crescent shape, rides on well ahead of the main body to signal back the first signs of the enemy. On this particular occasion I was one of the central pair – therefore the farthest forward – of this screen.

It was just getting dark when we set out and, after going but a few miles, our horses began stumbling and we found we were in a very heavy bog, the horses sinking in up to and over their knees. We passed the information back but were ordered to keep going, and so for half an hour or so the horses struggled on till at last we got on to firm ground. We rode on till we approached Ameysa, without drawing any enemy fire.

The squadron halted and a corporal and I were ordered to ride on through the grove to ascertain that it had been evacuated. What a pleasant thing to do! In pitch darkness, with just a sword for protection, to ride for something like half a mile through a thick palm grove in the middle of the desert with the chance of finding a Turk lurking behind every tree. That's how it sounded to us. At any rate, we rode on knee to knee, endeavouring to keep up a round of conversation. In some parts the trees were so thick we could hardly get through; weird and fantastic shapes fell across our path; everything was deadly quiet and still, and the sound of a snapping twig echoed through the stillness like the report of a rifle, causing us to take an even firmer grip on our swords. Our conversation became strained and finally ceased altogether.

At length, however, with a sigh of relief, we rode out into the open once more. But our task was not over yet, for now we had to ride right round the grove to scour the valley which surrounded it on three sides. We were able to report all clear, at which the squadron came up and we formed outposts all around the grove till morning and, after the early morning mists had cleared, we rode back to Katia.

Here we remained for only a few hours before moving on to Oghretina, which the Turks had now evacuated. While several of us were in search of firewood, we came across a dump of German and Turkish ammunition cases, on one of which was written in quite good English: 'Whoever shall first come to this spot Englishman, know that here was the telephone room connected with the guns which fired into your camps of Romani and Mohamadieh on August 4th.'

We spent the night at this grove and, at dawn the next day, set out again on the track of the Turks who were now holding a place called Bir el-ʾAbd a few miles away, and naturally were reinforced at each stage to which they retired. Here at Bir el-ʾAbd they put up quite a fierce resistance and fighting went on all day, incurring rather heavy casualties.

During the night we returned to Oghretina. The following morning we went out again to Bir el-ʾAbd and found the Turks had fallen back again to a place called Salmana, and from the top of a high ridge we could see shells exploding on the low ground in front of us, denoting that the Turks were still being pushed by other troops.

We patrolled in this neighbourhood all day without getting into direct action, finally returning to Oghretina that night. Here we remained for three whole days, a regiment of Australian Light Horse having taken our place in the forward push.

— *August 4th* —

The whole brigade was formed up outside the grove and the Brigadier General expressed his admiration at the manner in which we had carried out the hazardous duties of the past ten days. Better still, he informed us that we were now going down the line for a rest. Cigarettes were issued to every man and we felt that we were going on a real holiday. It was indeed a happy column of troops that moved off that morning and during the day wound its way across scorching hot sands, over ridges and along valleys, riding all day with an occasional break to rest or feed the horses.

Towards evening we came to Bir-el-Nusse, a little green patch in the midst of mountains of sand; the place where we had sunk wells some weeks previously.

Here we bivouacked for the night. Next morning saw us in the saddle again and we rode on to a place called Duiedar, where some of our troops had been in action with the enemy at Easter.

This was a palm grove of some considerable size and the terminus of a light railway, which ran from Khantara some five miles away, and this apparently was the end of our journey. The horse lines were fixed up on the edge of the grove and tents erected on the adjoining rising ground.

During our early days here we had a fairly easy time doctoring up our horses, many of which had received minor injuries, cleaning up our kit and equipment and renewing deficiencies. Later on, tactical schemes – mostly dismounted – and rifle-firing practice formed part of our daily routine, but on the whole we continued to have a fairly easy time.

7

HASSANIYA

About the middle of October, I contracted a mild attack of malaria and was in the sick lines when the regiment moved up the line again. Consequently I was ordered down to the base at Khantara for a month's rest. After about ten days, however, as the regiment needed reinforcements up the line, I went again and rejoined them at a palm grove called Hod el Fatia. The dates were now ripe and here we found some of the finest we had come across so far.

After a quick stay here we moved on a short distance to another spot called Hassaniya. Our arrival here marked the commencement of about a month of really strenuous and nerve-racking work, although no actual fighting took place.

Our camp was positioned some six or seven miles from railhead, in the midst of an endless stretch of sandy country which lay in ridges and valleys for miles around. As previously mentioned, the regiment consisted of three squadrons, and as one squadron at a time was out on patrol and outpost duty for about thirty-six hours at a time, there were never more than two squadrons in camp at the same time.

One of these squadrons had to provide a daily escort for the camel transport train to fetch forage and rations from railhead, and also provide three outposts for local protection every night. The routine for each squadron worked out somewhat as follows. Every man in camp had to stand to attention each morning; that is to say he had to have his horse saddled up with twenty-four hours' rations aboard, and be dressed in full marching order ready to move off at a minute's notice. (This was in case the Turks launched a surprise attack, and dawn was the most likely time for this to take place as it was invariably foggy at that time of day.) A patrol of one troop would then ride for several miles round the camp and if the all clear was called, we were allowed to off-saddle and the night outposts called in.

The men detailed for ration escort now had their breakfast and then started off to railhead. Often the ration train had not arrived by the time they did and there would be an indefinite wait. On its arrival, all the rations, forage and water (in tanks called 'fantasies') had to be unloaded and issued to the various units before we could start to load up the camels.

There would be perhaps forty or fifty camels in the convoy with one native in charge of perhaps four camels. A transport camel never moves at any great speed without cargo, but when loaded up with several sacks of barley, or a tank of water holding just over twelve gallons slung on each side of its saddle, its rate of progress is retarded further still. In some cases, where the load had not been evenly distributed, a camel would suddenly start careering round with a couple of cases of bully beef under its stomach instead of on its back, its driver almost frantic with excitement trying to get it to lie down while its load was readjusted. At any rate, in spite of these many little interludes, the convoy would invariably be safely escorted back to camp with its full quota of forage and rations.

On arrival in camp, the horses had to be unsaddled, rubbed down, watered and fed before we were permitted to draw our dinner from the cook house.

After dinner, we had to see to the horses again and get our saddles properly packed, ready for 'stand to' next morning.

At quarter to six in the evening, the night outposts had to fall in, dismounted this time, with blankets and groundsheet rolled into a neat bundle. Three outposts were mounted at different points round the camp with an NCO and three men on each post.

On arrival at the appointed spot, usually at the foot of a fairly high sand ridge, the first relief would be posted from six to eight in the evening. From the top of the ridge he would have a good view of the country for miles around. After dark he would periodically walk down the forward slope and listen for any suspicious sounds. At eight he would be relieved and return to the remainder of the party and soon get into his blankets for a few hours of sleep before his next tour of duty came round from midnight to two in the morning. So it went on throughout the night, with two hours on duty and four hours off, until the patrol had been out next morning and reported the all clear.

The first relief was not too bad as it was still daylight, but to be rudely awakened at midnight or two o'clock in the morning and roll out of a warm blanket to go and stand out there alone for two solid hours in the middle of the desert with eyes and ears strained to the limit was not so good. In the bright moonlight, bold black shadows were cast across the hills and valleys which, after endless gazing, would form into all manner of weird shapes. The cold, damp air would cause one's teeth to chatter. The eerie stillness and quiet would only be broken by the neighing of a horse back in camp. How slowly the minutes dragged along and how many an anxious glance at one's luminous Ingersoll watch seemed to show no alteration in the position of its hands. A thousand thoughts would come into one's mind, some to pass just as quickly as they came, others to linger on; how far away Blighty seemed – most thoughts led up to that.

Relief would come at last and, once again in the warm but now rather damp blankets, all evil thoughts of the two previous hours would soon pass away, and I may say that never was sleep so comforting or so refreshing as on these occasions, with the sands of the desert for a pillow and the stars above for a roof.

After the all clear had been given, the next morning we would return to camp and draw our breakfast. During the day we had numerous fatigue and camp duties, such as stable guards, mess orderly and pumping fatigue, which involved pumping water from a well into troughs for the horses. The night stable guard was mounted at six o'clock in the evening, with a corporal in charge of six men who worked in two-hour spells throughout the night, to see that no horses broke loose or became entangled in the ropes by which they were tethered.

About an hour before dawn, reveille sounded and the squadron would turn out to water and feed the horses, and then draw their own breakfast from the cookhouse. Following that, the order to saddle-up was given and, at dawn, the squadron would set out into the desert again to a spot called Homosieh which, like most of these desert objectives, was a palm grove nestling in a deep hollow surrounded on three sides by high sand ridges.

During the day, outposts were mounted on the ridges and patrols sent out to reconnoitre in all directions. A troop would probably be on outpost duty all morning and then sent out on patrol in the afternoon.

At night, the whole squadron would move out of the grove and form a continuous chain of outposts on the ridges surrounding it. After the exertions of the day and then to lie flat on one's stomach all night, peering and listening for any suspicious sound, it was most difficult to keep awake.

Dawn would break as a most welcome relief, and patrols would now be sent out again to reconnoitre. This would continue until the next squadron arrived during the morning to take over our duties. This particular duty came round in turn to each squadron every third day. This continual round of patrols, outpost duties, escorts and guards went on for weeks and during this time we got one night's rest in every three and that terminated an hour before dawn.

My first night's rest was marred by a severe attack of toothache and, being anxious not to waste any further chance of sleep, I reported sick next morning and briefly explained my trouble to the MO. He informed me that he had no proper instruments with him up the line, but that he could perform the necessary extraction if I could stand it.

After waiting while the other sick parade patients were attended to, the MO told me to sit down on a bully beef case outside his tent and, in a jiffy, the offending tooth was out. I returned happily and ate a jolly good breakfast.

Here, up the line, we had no tents to live in and had to build our own shelter with palm branches and anything else we could lay our hands on, which was not much. In most cases two men would work together and build a shack between them, and some weird-looking structures were erected. Fortunately, the weather remained fine and dry during our habitation of these shelters; otherwise I fear they would not have proved very serviceable.

— *November 25th* —

A little cheer went up when we were at last relieved and said goodbye to Hassaniya. In the late afternoon we struck the railway line (which was being pushed forward daily) at a point called Kherba, and there we bivouacked for the night. When we moved off again next morning it was a relief to find that we were heading down the line instead of in the opposite direction.

Before sunset we arrived back at Romani, where our troop remained while the rest of the regiment went further back still to Hill 70. We only remained here for a fortnight, but it was a fortnight which we always remembered as a very happy one. Apart from the usual stable and camp duties, our only job was to patrol the water pipeline twice daily. As only two men at a time were required for this patrol, the duty only came round to each pair once every fourth day.

The water pipe in question is worthy of mention because it carried fresh water from the base at Khantara, across the desert to a point some twenty-five miles away, and was being gradually pushed forward as the Turks were driven farther back until, eventually, the troops in Palestine were being supplied with fresh water from Egypt. Thus a prophecy of many years' standing was actually being fulfilled, for it had been prophesied that when the Nile flowed into Palestine its people would be delivered from the Turks.

— *December 9th* —

The regiment came up to Romani and we rejoined them. On the following day we commenced to travel up the line again, halting the first night at Kherba. Next day we went on to Bir-el-'Abd, where we remained for four days.

— *December 16th* —

We went on to Salmana and, after one night, went on to Mazar. Here we remained for one day's rest but, just as we were preparing our breakfast, an enemy plane came over and bombed us, one bomb dropping on the YMCA marquee.

— *December 18th* —

We moved on again as far as railhead which had now reached a point known as Kilo 128, that is to say, 128 kilometres from Khantara.

At eight o'clock that night I was ordered to saddle-up and report to brigade headquarters as a dispatch rider, and at two o'clock in the morning the whole brigade moved forward. At dawn we found ourselves quite close to the sea coast at a point called Bittieh, with El Arish only about five miles ahead. Here we remained in reserve to the Australian Light Horse who were attacking El Arish, and at about midday we received news that El Arish had fallen without much trouble. We therefore returned to Kilo 128, where I rejoined the regiment.

— December 20th —

Our troop and one other were ordered to saddle-up ready to escort a camel convoy up to El Arish. This convoy consisted of one thousand camels laden with forage, rations and water, with one native in charge of perhaps three or four camels – if you can imagine a thousand camels in single file you may picture the enormously long convoy which left Kilo 128 about midday that day.

Following the coastline we jogged along at a dreary pace for hour after hour. With the approach of darkness it became bitterly cold but still we jogged on, often walking beside our horse in an endeavour to keep warm. From our left came the continual dull roar of the sea; otherwise the eerie silence was only occasionally broken by the shrill cry of one of the native drivers to a camel which was lagging behind.

Just after midnight, when we had reached a point apparently opposite El Arish, which stood slightly inland, we halted and were met by a troop of Australians to whom we handed over the convoy with no regrets at all. We then bivouacked here on the beach and during the night there was a fall of snow.

— December 21st —

After a hasty breakfast of bully and biscuits, we saddled up and rode into El Arish. Here we took charge of Turkish prisoners who had been captured in the town and who were being temporarily kept in small parties of seven or eight in various buildings. Before long, our particular party made us understand that they wanted some water, so we ordered them to hand over their water bottles to one man so that he could be escorted to the source of supply. It fell to my lot to perform this escort duty to the wadi (valley), where the water was obtained about half a mile away.

On reaching the main square of the town, we found a procession of natives with their camels, goats, sheep and dogs parading round the square. A small group in the centre of the square beckoned and shouted for me to join the procession, which my prisoner and I did, to find that we had suddenly become film actors, for the procession was being photographed for a film company. However, we eventually arrived at the wadi, where my Turkish friend went about the filling the bottles rather too leisurely for my liking. Being unable to understand each other's language, a few bayonet prods were used to hurry him back to 'prison'.

During the afternoon, a company of infantry were brought up to take over the prisoners and so ended our police duties. Fortunately, however, I was lucky enough to drop in for another job in the town.

8

DISPATCHES

Just as we were about to return to the regiment, an order was received that an NCO and six men were to be left behind and report to Desert Column Headquarters as dispatch riders, and I was one of the six.

At headquarters it was explained that two men must always be on duty there, both day and night, but we could arrange among ourselves how we worked the reliefs.

The duties of the men on duty were to carry dispatches from headquarters and to pick up messages dropped by aeroplane. As the nearest aerodrome was something like a hundred miles away, many messages from GOC Headquarters were flown up here and dropped in a weighted bag with coloured streamers from the aircraft.

We soon arranged that each relief should be of four hours on duty, and eight hours off, and the first pair were posted immediately.

We fixed up the horse lines on the outskirts of the town within sight of headquarters, and when not on duty we slept in the open behind our horses. Eight hours off duty didn't mean we had nothing to do, for we had to do our own cooking, look after our horses and clean our saddlery and equipment. However, with no officer to boss us about, and with two men always on duty, there were never more than five horses on the lines at the same time and so we dispensed with stable guard altogether. It was just these little items which made us so happy with our present position.

December 24th (Christmas Eve)

Early this morning, my mate and I went on duty to relieve the two men who had done their four hours. Dispatches came through very frequently and we took it in turns to convey them to their respective destinations. At the end of four hours we were relieved and returned to our lines.

Although the weather was more like mid-summer in England, we intended to keep up the festival in the best English manner, and with this end in view bargained with one of the locals to sell us a couple of fowl which we had to purchase alive.

One man, a full-blooded Warwickshire farmer, soon had their necks screwed, after which we all gave a hand at plucking, and I volunteered to do the dressing. With a jackknife and bayonet the job was, if somewhat rudely, effectively carried out.

The next job was to try and scrounge vegetables, but the only thing we got from a raid on a small garden nearby was a few small carrots. However, we were quite satisfied and during the evening clustered round the camp fire, slowly quaffing our rum issue and, accompanied on the mouth organ, rent the desert air with a series of carols and all the old Blighty songs we could think of.

— December 25th (Christmas Day) —

The morning dawned as most mornings in that part of the world did; warm and bright. After breakfast, the general sent a message that he would like us to attend an open-air service which was to be held outside headquarters during the morning.

After a thorough wash, shave and general tidy up, we duly attended the service which we thoroughly enjoyed and appreciated. Following that, we immediately set about the preparations for our Christmas dinner. A large biscuit tin served as a stew-pot into which the two chickens and the carrots were placed. On a good fire the pot soon began to boil; noses were constantly pushed perilously close to the bubbling cauldron to inhale an aroma which, for so many months, had been so rare. At intervals a sword was jabbed into the pot to ascertain when the birds were ready for table.

At length it was decided that all was ready and so the meal commenced. First course was soup, which consisted of the water in which the birds had been cooked, together with the carrots. Then came the so-called chickens which, with bayonet and jackknife, were duly cut up and issued round as equally as possible.

Although it soon became evident that the chickens had seen more than one Christmas Day we, at any rate, enjoyed our feast and the desert dogs would find little meat on the bones which were eventually consigned to the dust heap.

At ten o'clock that night, my partner and I had to go on duty again. On night duty we were allowed to take a blanket with us so that we could lie down and have a nap behind our horses and, as messages came through, we were called by a messenger from the signal office.

About midnight I was called to take a dispatch to an Australian Brigade which had recently moved up to a spot 'somewhere near the coast.' That was the most precise indication of the actual position which they could give me. So I set out in the direction indicated, the stars being my only guide.

Practically the whole of the country, from the town itself to the coast, is a series of high sand hills amongst which I wandered about for an hour or more without finding any sign of an Australian camp at all. Consequently I returned to headquarters and reported the matter but was told that the dispatch was most important and must be delivered. So off I went again and was soon wandering among the sand hills, finally being caught up in some barbed-wire entanglements.

While endeavouring to extricate myself, I spotted a tent at the foot of the ridge below me. As there was a light in the tent I shouted out and immediately an Aussie came out and shouted directions as to my best way down to him. Fortunately this turned out to be the signal office of the brigade I wanted and so I immediately handed over my dispatch and started back to headquarters.

Of my exact position I had no idea but, guided by the stars, within about half an hour I was back in sight of headquarters on which a red light was kept burning at night. For the life of me, however, I could not find a way into the town. Every attempt I made led me into a cul-de-sac and from the dark shadows of the mud houses emerged dogs of all sizes sniffing and barking at my mare's heels. I must have ridden round the town several times without finding an entrance. It was now getting bitterly cold and, having smoked all my tobacco, I was utterly fed up and on the point of off-saddling and using the saddle blanket to wrap round me till daylight came, when I noticed my mare pulling in a certain direction. In a fit of despair I dropped the reins on her neck and said, 'Take me where you like,' and off she went. A few minutes later I was nearly thrown out of the saddle when she leapt over a trench, but a few minutes after that she had taken me straight back to our horse lines. Never before had I realised what a pal a horse could be.

— December 26th (Boxing Day) —

From the point of view of duties and general routine, the day was to us as any ordinary day. However, in the late afternoon, a hamper of Christmas fare was sent up to us from the regiment. This consisted of cold turkey, Christmas pudding, raw sausages and an extra rum issue and cigarettes.

As we had already had our dinner for that day from our rations, we decided to keep the eatables until the morrow and, as a means of keeping the sausages fresh, dug a hole in the sand, inserted a biscuit tin and placed the sausages inside it. Alas, next morning the sausages had gone. Evidently some of the desert dogs who had found so little on the chicken bones we left them the day before had sought their revenge!

A few days after Christmas the wet season set in with a vengeance and we were provided with billets in an empty mud house in the town. These so-called houses were only one storey high, and the fair-sized room which we were allocated was lighted only by a small lattice high up one of the walls and, of course, the place was totally unfurnished.

The door opened from a large square courtyard bounded on each of its four sides by houses similar to our own. On taking up residence here, we were naturally delighted to have a roof over our heads again. At bedtime we put down our blankets with pleasant anticipations of a peaceful night. Before long, however, everyone seemed to be restless, and my bed companion asked if I was feeling at all itchy. Itchy was not the word for it; I felt that all the fleas in Egypt were on a route march over my blankets.

Lighting a candle, we found that our blankets were literally alive with fleas, and it was evident that they were in too great numbers to be caught singly. Consequently we all took our blankets outside, gave them a jolly good shaking, searched our shirts for the stragglers – and there were many – and then made the best of a bad job till morning.

The matter was duly reported to the RAMC who came and thoroughly disinfected the house and all our blankets and equipment. This seemed to do the trick and we lived fairly comfortably for the next few days. Then one of our men was taken ill – diphtheria was diagnosed and he was sent off to hospital. Immediately after, several others began to feel ill and so we were all isolated. A troop of Australians were sent up to take over our duties; a pity, because this job suited us.

9

EL ARISH

— January 1st 1917 —

We were released from quarantine and rejoined the regiment, who were now at a point on the railway known as Kilo 139.

— January 4th —

We moved up to the outskirts of El Arish, where camp was pitched just beyond the town and not far from the coast. The horse lines had always been arranged in troop column, that is, each troop in single line one behind the other. Here, however, as there was a likelihood of enemy air raids, a different formation was adopted. Each squadron was arranged in one straight line at right angles to the next squadron so that the whole regiment eventually formed a large hollow square with the men sleeping behind their horses.

I mention this because during our very first night here it proved our salvation. Rolled up snugly in our blankets, we were suddenly awakened by a terrific crash followed immediately by another. Looking up we could see in the moonlight three or four enemy planes flying quite low over the camp, dropping bombs and firing their machine guns. The very ground rocked and it seemed that the whole camp must be blown to smithereens. Horses broke loose and galloped about frantically. We lay still, hoping for the best.

When at last the raid was over and the horses rounded up and sorted out again, we were astounded to find that the only casualties were a few wounded horses and no one had been killed. Most of the bombs had dropped inside the square and so burst almost harmlessly.

— January 8th —

We set out from El Arish on a 'stunt' which was successfully executed and of which we were for ever afterwards very proud.

About half past three in the afternoon, we started off with each man carrying twenty-four hours' rations of forage, bully and biscuits, and the regulation bottle of water which was not to be touched without orders. Apart from our own brigade (the 5th Mounted) of Warwicks, Worcesters and Gloucesters, the column consisted of the Camel Corps and a brigade of New Zealand Mounted Rifles supported by a battery of the HAC. Our job was to launch a surprise attack on the Turks at Rafah, which lay thirty miles away, at dawn on the Sunday.

Through the heat of the late afternoon and early evening we rode on over sand, sand and more sand. Puffing away at pipes and cigarettes, we were quite happy and gave little heed to the morrow.

With the arrival of darkness came that usual drop in the temperature; the dry warmth of the day giving place to a cold damp atmosphere, necessitating a halt to put on our greatcoats. Shortly after this we could tell from the actions of our horses that we were getting on to firmer ground and, as we proceeded, could see in the moonlight signs of vegetation and, in some places, even signs of cultivation, so we must be approaching the 'promised land'.

Still we plodded on, gradually getting more tired until about two o'clock in the morning, when we halted near the edge of a rather large palm grove called Sheik Zouwaid. Here we dismounted and fed our horses and were advised to lie down just as we were, beside our horses, and snatch an hour's sleep. No one suffered from insomnia!

Within a very short time, or so it seemed, we were in the saddle again, quite refreshed, pushing on over the remaining five miles or so to Rafah and Palestine.

After about an hour's ride we halted and were ordered to dismount. As dawn broke, we found ourselves sheltered and hidden in a large natural depression somewhat resembling a saucer, in which we could see no farther than the rim. Several of our planes were flying overhead and several messages were dropped by them.

At last came the order to mount and, as we rode over the edge of the saucer, the sight that met our eyes almost caused us to forget the Turks, for there lay a wide expanse of flat country covered with grass. To eyes which had witnessed nothing like this since leaving England, it was indeed a tonic. However, less than a mile ahead, the ground rose into a stiff ridge, the near side of which was strongly fortified by the Turks; trenches, redoubts and barbed-wire entanglements forming part of the defences.

Once over the edge, little puffs of smoke and cracking shrapnel let us know that the action had started. Orders were then given rapidly: 'Draw swords. Form column of half-squadrons. Trot.'

We were now crossing the green plain straight for the enemy positions from which rifle and machine gun fire was directed at us. 'Gallop!' and away we went when suddenly we were signalled to halt, followed by the orders: 'Return swords. Action front dismount.'

At this order, three men out of every four dismount and hand over their horses to the fourth man and then lie down flat to await the next order.

The horses are then galloped back to cover while the dismounted men move forward in an extended line by short rushes of ten or twelve yards at a time. Thus, over that stretch of open ground with no cover whatsoever, we gradually advanced under fire until close enough to the enemy to take fairly accurate aim with our rifles.

Fortunately, our own battery soon silenced some of the enemy artillery which was a great relief to us. For some four or five hours we kept up a steady fire on the enemy positions which, apparently, were more strongly held than had been anticipated.

We were ultimately ordered to crawl back some distance while our horses were brought up to us. As soon as the horses appeared very heavy fire was directed at us and, though it did not take us long to get mounted and gallop out of range, many casualties occurred.

As I was about to mount, I suddenly had a feeling that I was going to get hit and instantly pulled my mare between me and the enemy. At that moment, a bullet zipped into my great coat which was rolled up and strapped onto the front of the saddle.

As we galloped out of action, many riderless horses were galloping about loose – a sure sign of casualties. However, the survivors quickly reformed and we were then rushed across to the left flank, where a range of sand dunes skirted the battlefield. From here the dismounted attack was resumed, but again fate was very kind to me, as it turned out. As we galloped across to this new position, the troop officer turned round in his saddle and, as I was the first person he noticed, shouted to me to take a message back to headquarters, which I did. By the time I rejoined the squadron, many casualties had taken place. The squadron leader and his servant were both wounded and my particular pal, who had been beside me all day, lay with a bad wound to his chest. Another pal from Nuneaton, Os Pallett, was wounded in the thigh and lay with various other casualties, many of which had been caused by snipers in the dunes.

The attack was pushed forward and, just as daylight faded, a mighty cheer went up; Rafah had fallen, along with – as we later learnt – over two thousand prisoners, four field guns and numerous machine guns.

The wounded were collected and placed in sand carts with very broad tyres, and others were placed on stretchers slung on either side of a camel. The horses were then brought up and we prepared for the thirty-mile return trek to El Arish. Some idea of the casualties sustained may be formed from the fact that every man was leading at least one riderless horse and many were leading two.

With the sad thoughts of so many missing comrades, a monotonous ride of thirty miles in front of us and tired out almost to the point of exhaustion, it was a very quiet and gloomy column of troops that turned its back on Rafah that night.

After about an hour's ride, when most of us were on the point of falling asleep in our saddles, we passed through a scattered palm grove and, on the far side, were agreeably surprised to see a number of candle lights, in the flickering gleams of which we could distinguish a party of men and camels. This, then, was Sheik Zouwaid and the party in question had brought up water and rations for us.

Water was the first cry of all, and then we were issued with bully beef and biscuits and a good tot of rum and condensed milk. Meanwhile, the horses were watered and given the remainder of the feed which we carried on our saddles. Our spirits quickly rose and after about an hour's rest it was a much merrier column that moved off on the remaining twenty-five miles to El Arish.

For a time we smoked, chatted over the events of the day and even broke out into occasional song as we rode along through the damp, dark, dreary hours, but we were too tired to keep this up for long. At the end of every half-hour or so, we halted to rest the horses for five minutes, and each time more than half the regiment was asleep before that time was up. Even as we rode along, quite frequently horses from the rear would come walking along the column with the rider fast asleep.

At one point when we halted, I was astonished not to recognise any of the men near me. Discreet enquiries elicited the information that I was not even in my own squadron, let alone the right troop. Apparently I had fallen asleep and my mare, with no restraining hand, had worked her way almost to the head of the column. In the darkness it was no easy matter to find my proper place again. So many other men, like me, had fallen asleep and were not in their proper places, making my task slightly more difficult.

Half-hour followed half-hour for what seemed like an eternity, until dawn began to break and, although we were still some miles from camp, the approach of daylight roused us up somewhat. Then, at about six in the morning, the minarets of El Arish became visible in the distance and seemed to give us a new lease of life. About an hour later we made quite a lively entrance into camp.

Horses were immediately unsaddled, watered and fed and we, after a breakfast of porridge and bacon, were allowed several hours' sleep. Considering that during the past forty hours we had ridden something like sixty miles and fought a successful action lasting fourteen or fifteen hours, we felt that those few hours of sleep had been well earned. The remainder of the day was spent chiefly in sorting out the horses and saddlery which, as may be imagined, had become somewhat mixed up during the proceedings of the previous day.

— January 11th —

I received the sad news that my pal, who had been wounded in the chest, had died during the night in the field hospital. This was indeed a sad blow to all of us, for he had been one of the best-hearted and cheeriest men in the regiment.

For many months he and I had lived together. The night before the action, we had slept together under the same blankets; we had ridden side by side to Rafah and, side by side, had gone into the action which had cost him his life. At the suggestion of the troop sergeant it was arranged that his closest friends should form a funeral party to give him at least a soldier's burial. So, on the following afternoon, we sadly escorted the gun-carriage, its grim burden covered with the Union Flag, from the field hospital to the little desert cemetery which, as yet, had witnessed but few of these sad ceremonies. The burial rites were performed by the chaplain, the Last Post was sounded and a small wooden cross erected as testimony to the fact that one of England's sons had done his duty.

A week or two later we moved a little further up the line to a place called El Burg, where we were chiefly engaged on patrols and outpost duties. On several occasions we were sent out to the flank to round up certain Bedouin tribes who were alleged to be giving information to the enemy. On the first of these outings we rounded up a whole tribe as they were moving quietly through a deep valley with their camels, donkeys, goats, dogs etc. It was a slow job escorting this motley assembly along the seven or eight miles back to camp, and our progress on this occasion was further delayed owing to the fact that one of the women in the tribe gave birth on the way.

Most of our spare time here was spent playing football, a game encouraged throughout the regiment. The firmest strip of ground available was actually part of one of the old caravan routes from Egypt to Palestine, whose surface had been trodden hard by the feet of camels over the centuries. This formed an ideal football ground, as it was bounded on two sides by high sand ridges which made a natural grandstand for the spectators. Every troop was called on to form a team and I was elected captain of our troop. Matches were played almost every afternoon and highly exciting games they were.

In the midst of this however, our troop and one other were sent back to El Arish where railhead had now been established. Here we lived under canvas again, very cosily, and our only duty was to draw the regiment's forage and rations from railhead each morning and escort the camel convoy which carried them up to El Burg. This only lasted for a fortnight, after which we rejoined the regiment and almost immediately moved forward to Sheikh Zouaid. We were now almost on the threshold of Palestine, where we should come on hard ground and metal roads again.

During the past fifteen months, while crossing the sandy desert, the horses had not carried shoes on their hind feet and consequently now had to be fully shod. The shoeing-smiths had a very busy time of it but, by working almost all day and night, the job was accomplished in remarkably quick time.

Whatever work was carried out here was, at any rate, screened from the enemy eyes for, during the whole time, a *khamsin* or *sirocco* was in progress (this is a hot, dry wind bringing with it a continuous cloud of dust and sand, quite obliterating the sun and daylight and causing a suffocating sensation).

Two other events which happened here are worth recording; one was the arrival of reinforcements from England and the return to the regiment of some of the men who had been wounded at Rafah; the other event was 'fumigation', or as it was more popularly called, 'Louse Parade'.

The procedure for this went somewhat as follows: one squadron at a time paraded with their blankets and, all wearing apparel, rode to the nearest point on the railway which was being pushed forward daily. On arrival here we had to strip, roll all our belongings into a bundle and, after attaching our identity disc thereto, deposit our bundle in a closed railway truck. The doors of the truck were then closed and apparently the massacre commenced.

While this was proceeding, we had to jump one by one into a ballast truck of disinfectant. This was quite refreshing and, in any case, helped to pass away the time until our clothes came out again.

When at last the truck doors were opened again, the steaming hot bundles were forked out with a long pole into a heap. It was a proper pantomime trying to find one's own steaming bundle again; we found tunics and breeches creased almost out of recognition and everything was strongly pervaded with that 'suits cleaned and pressed' odour. A leather purse (empty!) that I had left in one of my tunic pockets crumbled to pieces at the first touch after its baking, which gave some idea of the stringent treatment meted out in the process. None but the most stubborn louse could survive such treatment but, within a few days, we had reason to believe that some of the stoutest were attached to the regiment.

10

FIRST ATTACK ON GAZA

Early in March we moved up to Rafah and the welcome green slopes of that part of Palestine.

From the fact that the tents and all superfluous equipment were left behind, we knew that the immediate future was going to bring activity again. Consequently, and with no surprise, a few days later we found ourselves in the saddle before dawn, setting out to reconnoitre the enemy positions at and around Gaza, which lay some eight or nine miles away.

By dawn we were riding through fields, more like prairies of barley, still green and waving in the slight breeze. I was once again part of the advance screen moving forward in pairs some half-mile ahead of the brigade.

Our instructions were to head for a very high horseshoe-shaped mound which could then be dimly seen in the far distance. About midday we came up to this huge mound – Tel el Jemmi – and found it was situated on the side of a very deep and wide wadi, the Wadi Ghuzze. The far side of the mound had been cut out almost perpendicularly by the rush of water along the wadi during the wet seasons. To our left we knew that the wadi ran into Gaza, and to the right we supposed it ran somewhere into the neighbourhood of Beersheba. However, the brigade halted at the foot of the mound and patrols were sent out across the wadi to reconnoitre from the top of a ridge some half a mile on the far side.

We were now in enemy country and likely to draw fire at any moment. At any rate, we proceeded cautiously to the top of the ridge and nothing happened. From here we could see into Gaza on our left. Presently we heard artillery fire. The little puffs of smoke that followed told us that the patrols directly in front of Gaza were now drawing fire.

Two of us were now ordered to ride forward until we drew rifle fire. We must have got close to an enemy outpost before this happened, at which we galloped back and reported. Outposts were then posted at various points and the patrols returned to the main body across the wadi.

During a few leisure hours in the afternoon, we found a wonderful array of wild flowers. To us, who had spent so long crossing the desert, they seemed more wonderful than any flowers in cultivation. Many of these flowers were carefully picked and, at a later date, sent home to relatives and friends in England.

After watering the horses at a small well near the wadi, we started back to Rafah at four in the afternoon. Before we had gone far, however, rifle fire was heard in the rear and we found that our rear guard had been intercepted by a Turkish cavalry patrol. Fortunately it was only a small patrol and our men were able to get through without any casualties.

About an hour later we saw an aeroplane flying very low away to our left but, thinking it was one of our own, paid no particular attention to it until it suddenly came towards us, swooped down and emptied its machine gun into the column. We immediately extended but the firing went on until apparently the ammunition ran out. Strange to relate; the only casualty was a man in my troop who was leading the pack mule. He was wounded in the thigh, the bullet burying itself in the flesh. This meant a very painful ride of several hours back to Rafah where he was taken to the field hospital and next morning sent down the line to the hospital train. This hospital train, composed of all white coaches surmounted with the Red Cross, became known from its picturesque appearance as 'The Queen of the Desert'.

During the past few weeks there had been much activity all along the lines of communication. The railway had been pushed forward as far as possible, great dumps of forage and rations had come into being at many points, and guns of every calibre and battalions of infantry and RAMC units had gone forward up the line. Aeroplanes had been continually buzzing backwards and forwards overhead and we had numerous kit and arms inspections. These were all items in preparation for the pending attack on Gaza which, it was very evident, was to be carried out on a much larger scale than any of our previous actions. Operations were also to be on a much wider front than before, extending from the high sand dunes along the coast, across undulating country broken in unexpected places by wadis of various sizes, of which the Wadi Ghuzze was the largest and most important. Consequently I can only describe the more or less minor parts of the engagement, that is, the part which we ourselves were deputed to carry out, as of course we knew little of what was actually happening on other parts of the front.

— March 19th —

Our share in the battle commenced early on this morning, when the whole brigade rode out of Rafah in full marching order. Gradually heading for the sand dunes which ran along the coast, we followed these until about three o'clock in the afternoon, by which time we were some four or five miles from Gaza. Here we halted and tethered the horses and, after receiving detailed instructions regarding the pending operations, were allowed to go for a bathe in the sea.

We remained at this spot until about half past two in the morning, when reveille was sounded, after which the horses were watered and fed and we ourselves partook of a service breakfast of bread and bully beef.

At around three o'clock in the morning we moved off but, as we appeared to be turning first right and then left, it was almost impossible to know exactly in which direction we were going.

By dawn it was very foggy and we found ourselves close to Tel el Jemmi, where columns of infantry were moving up to their positions. We crossed the wadi and proceeded for some small distance on the far side before halting.

As daylight broadened, the gradually increasing warmth of the sun dispersed the fog and the whole country was again bathed in brilliant sunshine. The whole of the cavalry was being used on the flanks, both as guard to the infantry and for the purpose of holding up any Turkish reinforcements which might attempt to get through to Gaza.

From this point our troop – about thirty men – under the command of the troop officer, were sent forward to keep a watch on the enemy redoubts at Sheria, which lay, as we approached, to the right of Gaza.

Riding in pairs, with some twenty-yard intervals between each pair, we went forward, and very soon occasional shells from a long-range gun began to fall uncomfortably close to us, but mostly passing overhead. The gun itself must have been at some considerable distance because the report of the gun did not reach us until after the shell had burst. The shells were being fired at regular intervals of about five minutes. We continued to go forward, however, and for the greater part of the day manoeuvred in front of the enemy redoubts, on one occasion galloping right across their front, thereby drawing rifle and machine gun fire.

All day long the shells were bursting with irritating regularity behind us, while we attracted the attention of the troops at Sheria, who made no attempt to leave their stronghold. In the late afternoon we returned to the brigade who had remained (all day) where we left them in the morning. However, they had received various casualties. One of the shells which had been passing over us had dropped right in the middle of our squadron, killing outright our squadron leader and seriously wounding others.

As dusk was descending, we received a sudden order to mount and gallop into action on our extreme right. Coming into action on a fairly high ridge, the Turks got us nicely with their guns, the shells bursting all around us. Across the lower lying ground we could see Turkish infantry advancing in great numbers from the direction of Beersheba. For the greater part of the night we held them off, but very suddenly came the order, 'Get back to your horses!' then, in quick succession, 'Mount. Trot. Gallop!' apparently only just in the nick of time – we later learnt that in another five minutes the whole regiment would have been surrounded.

It was still dark, but as we began to descend a fairly stiff ridge, several isolated lights became visible. Soon, we passed a bell tent, inside which a lighted candle showed up the outline of a large red cross painted on the outside of the canvas. Outside the tent lay a row of stretchers, from several of which issued groans of agony; and beyond the stretchers a long row of blanketed forms from which no sound would ever escape again.

Dawn found us still in the saddle riding back for water, and at about eight o'clock we arrived at a small native village called Deir el Belah, fairly close to the spot which we had started out from the previous day.

By this time, horses and men were craving water, which we found at a small well in the village. Then we received the news that the action of the previous day had been unsuccessful, and that the Turks still held Gaza. Consequently, instead of a short rest which we had anticipated, we had to stand to arms, not being allowed to unsaddle or remove any equipment all day long, ready to move anywhere at a moment's notice.

At dusk we moved out to the flank, forming a line of outposts till morning. As a matter of fact, we spent almost a month patrolling and forming outposts day after day and night after night. In the saddle all day and on outpost duty all night with never a chance of removing one's equipment, leave alone one's clothes and not more than four hours sleep at a stretch. This was one of the most tedious periods of our active service career so far.

During a short rest at Belah, the brigade was issued with Hotchkiss guns, one gun to each troop. Consequently, gun teams had to be selected, four men to each gun, and I was one of the four selected for our troop.

The Hotchkiss gun was actually an automatic rifle, easily transported, and was to the cavalry what the Lewis gun was to the infantry. It fired ordinary .303 rifle ammunition, which was fed into the gun from metal strips, each holding 30 rounds. It was capable of firing a strip of 30 rounds at the rate of 200 rounds per minute. A very useful weapon, and, naturally, its somewhat intricate mechanism necessitated long, careful and (to us) painful instruction regarding its action and movements. Consequently, we gunners spent many weary hours mastering the actual working of the gun, including assembling, stripping, loading, firing and, most important of all, stoppages – there was also to be learnt the important operation of getting the gun into and out of action.

Though having to learn everything about the gun, each man in the tent was allotted his own particular job:

- No. 1 was the corporal who was responsible for carrying the gun into action and for doing the actual firing, so he carried the spare parts bag.
- No. 2 (that was me) was responsible for loading the gun, changing the barrel when necessary, picking up targets and directing fire. Consequently, No. 2 carried the spare barrel slung in a case on his back, a pair of field glasses and, on going into action, two cases of ammunition.
- No. 3 was essentially the ammunition man, always taking into action two

cases of ammunition, but remaining behind Nos 1 and 2 as a connecting file between the gun and the team's horses.

- No. 4 had the job of looking after the horses whenever the team went into action. A good No. 4 was a great asset, particularly at times when it was necessary to make a hasty retreat.

The gun, spare barrel and ammunition (in five leather cases, each holding 6 strips of 30 rounds) were carried on a packhorse which, of course, No. 4 had to lead. Each member of the team also carried two small pouches of ammunition, each containing three strips of 30 rounds, strapped to the front of his saddle.

Having stated these particulars, it may sound a simple operation to take the gun into action, but a short description of one of our early practise runs will explain, to some extent, the many pitfalls which we encountered.

Imagine the gun team out at practise one morning, riding sedately abreast behind the troop officer who suddenly turns round and shouts, 'We are going to get the gun into action on that ridge in front. Trot. Canter. Gallop.'

Suddenly, the packhorse starts a wild stampede and No. 4 finds that we have dropped a case of ammunition and that two others are hanging loose under the horse's belly. Unconscious of what has happened, the officer gallops on but the team halts to retrieve the ammunition.

The officer arrives at the foot of the ridge alone. Galloping back to us he shouts, 'What the hell are you doing, corporal?'

The corporal, red in the face and wet with perspiration, explains, all the while cursing No. 2 (who has now returned with the fallen ammunition case) for not strapping the cases on securely.

At length off we go again and, having arrived at the foot of the ridge, receive the orders, 'Action front dismount.'

Nos 1, 2 and 3 hurriedly dismount but, in handing over their horses to No. 4 who remains mounted, get in each other's way. Meanwhile, the packhorse twists and turns in all directions, eventually becoming entangled in the reins of the other horses. All the while No. 4 is cursing us all for causing such a mix-up.

In the end, the job is straightened out but, instead of taking a matter of seconds, has taken something like three or four minutes.

At length, No. 1 gets his gun down and proceeds to mount the ridge, followed immediately by No. 2 who, incidentally, slips down in the loose sand and gets the spare barrel choked up with sand.

The gun is eventually mounted on the crest of the ridge and the officer, who is notoriously short-sighted, prepares to give the fire order somewhat as follows: 'Load,' at which the gun is loaded with the first strip of dummy ammo. 'Immediate front, isolated palm tree; three o'clock short cactus hedge at near end of which is a large bird; open fire.'

The corporal at once replies, 'That isn't a bird sir, it's the sergeant.'

The officer replies, 'Well open fire quick or he'll be gone!'

Several other targets are in turn described, if not always recognised, when the officer says, 'You are now supposed to have fired 500 rounds so change the barrel, and remember, the barrel is now nearly red-hot.'

Out comes No. 2's handkerchief with which to handle the barrel, but knowing the spare barrel is choked up with sand, puts the old one back again. In an endeavour to conceal this movement, he has had to crawl slightly forward. The officer, noticing this, calls out, 'No. 2 do you know you are in full view of the enemy, and also in front of the muzzle of your own gun! Get back, damn you!'

After a few other words of advice we get the order, 'Out of action.' The gun is therefore unloaded and carried away by No. 1, with No. 2 following on his heels. No. 3, in his hurried flight, has omitted to fasten up one of his ammunition cases with the result that the strips are falling out as he runs along. No. 2 shouts out to tell him of this, at the same time picking up some of the strips himself. By the time Nos 2 and 3 have got back to their horses, the corporal has replaced the gun on the packhorse and remounted his own horse.

While Nos 2 and 3 are replacing their particular items on the pack saddle, it is discovered that the spare parts bag is missing. This, of course, is the responsibility of the corporal, so he has to dismount again and chase up the ridge in search of the missing satchel. He finds it where the gun had been mounted and hastily returns to a frowning officer and three grinning members of his gun team.

Needless to say, the officer calls us a proper lot of duds and threatens to have us out at further practise at every possible opportunity. By the time we get back to camp, however, we forget all about gun practise and don't much care if we lose the whole outfit as long as we get our dinner.

11

SECOND ATTACK ON GAZA

About the middle of April we set out from Belah on the second attack on Gaza. As on the previous occasion, we were again operating on the flank, but the Turks had now established a more or less continuous line of defence, right from Gaza to Beersheba. Immediately after crossing the main wadi, we were greeted with persistent shellfire but, opening out to battle order, we pushed forward until we reached a smaller wadi at a point called Erk. Here we dismounted and, leaving the horses sheltered in the wadi, advanced on foot for some distance, eventually forming an extended line on both sides of the wadi at right angles to it.

Although being under intermittent fire, we had not so far seen the enemy. My duty as No. 2 was, as previously mentioned, to endeavour with the aid of field glasses to pick up suitable targets. At regular intervals, bullets kept 'flipping' dangerously close to our gun; this led us to believe that we were being sniped. After a very careful survey of the ground in our immediate front, I suddenly caught a momentary glimpse of something red disappearing below ground at a range estimated to be four or five hundred yards.

Keeping my glasses glued to this spot, I saw two heads wearing red fez caps appear above the ground; two rifles were raised and a few shots fired before the two heads immediately disappeared again. So cleverly was the hiding place concealed (no sign of loose earth having been thrown up) that it was almost impossible to pick out with the naked eye. With the aid of glasses I was able to direct our fire fairly accurately. This had the effect of keeping our friends quiet for longer intervals, but we failed to silence them completely.

In the afternoon, the firing on our immediate front died down considerably until, at about four o'clock, a large body of Turkish infantry suddenly appeared, advancing at the double in mass formation. Not a shot was fired until they got within about three hundred yards of us and then machine guns, Hotchkiss guns and rifles opened fire simultaneously and the Turks went down like ninepins. Those that were able turned and fled as hard as they could.

We held on here till dark and then returned to our horses in the wadi and started back for water to a place called El Menduh. Arriving here at about nine in the evening we were not allowed to water but were ordered on to Tel el Jemmi, which lay some three or four miles off. On arrival we were told that our watering place was at El Menduh, where water had just been refused to us. After some time had been spent in arguments we set off again on the return to El Munduh. Having covered about half the distance, we were again stopped and ordered back to Jemmi. As you may imagine, some very uncomplimentary remarks were now being passed about the British Army in general. However, we were finally allowed to water at Jemmi. It was a long job as the wells, by this time, had run almost dry and water filtered in very slowly. To cap the lot, as soon as we had watered the horses we had to return to El Menduh for the night, but it was now nearly five o'clock in the morning and, worse still, we were greeted with the news that Gaza still remained in the hands of the Turks.

After tethering the horses we got down to a few hours of sleep, but early the next morning we were rather heavily bombed by enemy planes that caused a fair amount of damage. The failure of the Gaza operation meant that we were immediately sent out on patrol and outpost duties, and were thus employed for some considerable time until relieved by the Australian Light Horse. We then returned to Belah for a rest which was of a very brief duration, for we were soon sent out to a place called Shellal. This was merely another large horseshoe-shaped mound on the back of the wadi, similar to Jemmi.

On a rising piece of ground about a mile from and overlooking the wadi, we were set to dig trenches and form a redoubt complete with barbed wire entanglements. This was real hard work in such a climate and especially at this time of year. To make things worse, when the redoubt was complete, one of the 'heads' thought it would be a good idea to have the Hotchkiss guns out in front, beyond the wire entanglements. Consequently, we poor gunners had to dig a sap out under the wire and, at the end, dig an emplacement for the gun sufficiently deep for the gunners to stand upright when firing the gun.

One strange thing about our present position was that the water lay in the wadi between ourselves and the Turks, so that when watering the horses we had to go armed. Apparently a strong counter-attack was expected, but fortunately it did not happen while we were here, if ever it did happen. At any rate, we were eventually relieved and sent down to Marakeb which is on the coast just behind Belah. Here we spent a very happy fortnight living in 'bivvies', which we soon constructed from any material at hand. Fairly light duties, plenty of bathing and a neighbouring canteen made life quite happy and joyful again.

At the end of a fortnight we were sent out to a very wild and dreary spot called Abassan-tel-el-Kebir. It was a terribly dusty place; even a column of horses going to water was sufficient to stir up a cloud of dust so thick that it was impossible to see many yards ahead, with the result that both men and horses were white over in a very few minutes. The unpleasantness was further intensified as we experienced several khamsins while here.

Several minor stunts were carried out, one of which was to escort and cover a party of Royal Engineers while they blew up one of the enemy's bridges.

Under cover of darkness we got through the Turkish lines and up went the bridge, quite unknown to the Turks.

Towards the end of May we were sent over to occupy a line of redoubts close to the one we had erected at Shellal. Several weeks were spent here; as a matter of fact, we were still here when General Allenby came out to take over the command of the Egyptian Expeditionary Force.

Soon after his arrival we were sent out on several occasions to reconnoitre as far away as Khalasa, which is not many miles from Beersheba, and lies amongst some very wild and treacherous hill country.

These jobs of probing the enemy positions were not too pleasant as we had to invite the enemy to open fire on us to ascertain the strength of his various positions. However, towards the end of June, the regiment was ordered back to Marakeb for a rest, but a certain number of men were selected from each troop to form a composite squadron to parade before General Allenby on the following day, as he was already up the line inspecting the various units under his command. I was one of the men selected for this parade, and on the following morning came face-to-face with the commander who was so soon to lead us to victories which, on past occasions, had been failures. It may have been the brief and informal manner in which he addressed us, but one and all immediately formed a very high opinion of our new CIC.

With the parade over, we set off right away for Marakeb to rejoin the regiment. After the first few days here, which were chiefly spent in overhauling our saddlery and equipment, we had a real good time. The weather was now at its hottest, so that practically all our duties were performed before breakfast each day. Each morning we went bathing in the sea and most afternoons the horses were taken into the water for a bathe too. In addition to this, an occasional arms or saddlery inspection were about the only parades we had to attend.

1 On June 28th, 1915, Cady joined the Machine Gun Corps of the Warwickshire Yeomanry.

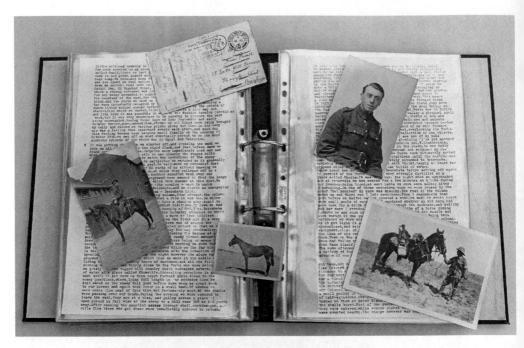

Above 2 The original diary of Cady Cyril Hoyte. (Courtesy R. Elverstone)

Left 3 Horse and rider – 164684 Pte Hoyte.

4 Tidworth Training Camp stables, September 5th, 1915. Cady is holding the shovel.

5 Horse and rider with full equipment.

Left 6 Date Palm. In November 1915, Cady was sent overseas where he fought as part of the British Expeditionary Force in Egypt.

Below 7 'Our Tent' at Hill 70, July 1916. From left to right: Baker, Smith, Cady, Oliver, Minett, Locke, Coleman (corporal).

8 Oliver and his pal 'at home' in camp at Tel el Marakeb.

9 First halt in Palestine near Tel el Jemmi.

10 Oghretina, August 1916.

11 Duiedar, August 1916.

12 Sea bathing at Marakcb.

13 Grave of Jack Northover at El Arish.

14 'Home-built shacks'.

15 Kantara, June 1916.

Left 16 Prison at Alexandria, with the scaffold showing on roof.

Below 17 Censored postcard dated January 17th, 1916. Sent from Cady to his brother Francis while on active service: 'Just to let you know I am still alright.' He signs it with his middle name, Cyril.

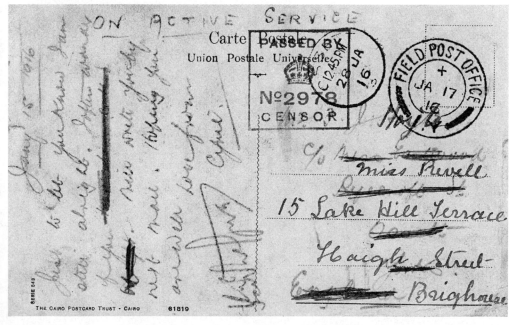

18 Hospital ship on the Suez Canal, Ballah, April 1916.

19 The wadi near Tel-el Farrar.

20 A signaller
off duty.

21 Bedouins rounded
up as spy suspects.

22 Turkish
prisoners
captured at Rafa,
January 1917.

23 Beersheba.

24 Some members of the
British Secret Service.

25 Egyptian Mounted Police.

26 Khan Yunis.

27 Bedouin group.

28 Kantara.

29 Bedouins drawing water at a well in Beersheba.

Above 30 A group of Bedouins.

Right 31 Cady with his son Granville John (known as 'Jack'). After the war, Cady married May Saunders and worked as a textile manufacturer's agent with Messrs Hall and Phillips Ltd.

32 Cady lived in London during his retirement. A quiet, peaceful man with a good sense of humour, Cady enjoyed fishing and was a keen gardener, winning prizes for his sweet peas. Cady passed away in 1969, followed by his wife May in 1978 and son Jack in 2005.

12

PORT SAID

Men were now granted leave again, four men from each squadron each week, with the choice of Alexandria, Cairo or Port Said. In each case a free railway warrant was issued. At Cairo and Alexandria it was necessary to fix up and pay for one's own accommodation, whereas at Port Said it was possible to stay at the Australian Rest Camp where food and accommodation were provided free of charge.

Previously when leave had been permitted, I had always refused to take it, saying that I would wait till I could go to Blighty. By now my name was first on the leave list and, having spent something like twenty months up the line, I decided to take ten days' leave at Port Said.

— July 28th —

The four leave men rode light-heartedly out of camp, across to the railway at Khan Yunis, which was our nearest station, and there handed over our horses to be taken back to camp.

At about half past six in the evening the train arrived, just open goods trucks, and was already well packed with troops from other units. We, however, managed to scramble in and, after a bit of a sing-song, managed to get our blankets down on the floor of the truck and so slept through the night.

Arriving at Khantara at about six in the morning, we were provided with breakfast and then marched across the pontoon bridge to Khantara West Station.

After a rather long wait here, we eventually boarded another goods train which landed us in Port Said at about quarter to one in the afternoon. Straight through the town we marched to the rest camp on the beach but, before entering, had to hand in our blankets and were issued with brand new ones. The camp commandant read out orders to the effect that, each morning there would be a rifle inspection at nine-thirty in the morning, after which there would be no further restrictions whatsoever.

Officially we were expected to be back in camp by midnight, but nothing would be said if we were out later. We were, of course, to live under canvas, but the tents were pitched right on the beach so that we could get straight out of bed in the morning and go for a dip. Plenty of good army food was provided and we were allowed to go to the quartermaster's stores at certain times each day to draw whatever new clothing we required.

In the camp was a large YMCA marquee where light refreshments could be obtained at any time, writing materials provided and, in fact, all those little extras for which the YMCA was always a magnet to the troops.

Farther along the beach was the Empire Club, where bathing costumes could be hired, refreshments obtained and there was a good supply of papers and periodicals at one's disposal. Here, after a bathe, one could sit in a comfortable wicker chair, sipping iced lemonade, leisurely reading the *Tatler* or *Bystander*, or lazily gazing up at the monument of Ferdinand de Lesseps, which stood nearby at the entrance to the canal which brought him fame.

In the town were numerous cafés and restaurants, chiefly French and Italian, and shops of all kinds from the modern European stores to the humble little native bazaar. The coinage in circulation was, like the population, most cosmopolitan. Egyptian piasters, French and Belgian francs were perhaps most common, but all English coins, together with German marks, Italian lira and Indian rupees were met with everywhere. Half-crowns were no better than florins for converting here for, with such a varied coinage in circulation, it was a work of art counting one's change, especially after changing a 50 or 100 piaster note, and the natives were not slow in realising this.

In the centre of the town were two cinemas, a Church Army Rest Centre and a Salvation Army Rest. At this latter we spent an hour or so each day playing Ping-Pong. Here in Port Said, we had a good opportunity of studying more closely the habits of the population, which ranged from the Egyptians to the Sudanese. The Egyptians claimed two things; a pedigree older than the pyramids, and a shrewd business sense.

The Sudanese was the fellow with the best heart of all. Invariably a fine specimen of manhood, fairly treated, would prove a staunch friend through thick and thin.

A quaint, yet ofttimes aggravating figure always well to the fore, was the little shoe blacker who plied his trade with a fleet hand but with a fleeter and still more subtle tongue. He would always accept a piaster but never a refusal. He was a jolly little chap who, if he cheated you for a piaster, left you feeling that he had earned it by his ready wit and audacity.

As in Cairo, the whole place seemed wrapped in an atmosphere of drowsiness; no hustle or bustle, but just a sense of everything drifting along to its own pre-destined termination. It is, I think, this very atmosphere which is at once seductive that gives the East its strange indescribable lure.

It is unnecessary to give a detailed account of each day's happening, but a rough idea of one of our typical days will suffice. I was one of three pals who spent practically all our time together. After the morning rifle inspection we would saunter along the beach to the Empire Club. Invariably we would spend anything up to an hour in the quite warm water of the Mediterranean Sea, and then partake of light refreshments at the club instead of going back to camp for the midday meal. Sometimes, for a change, we would go to the Salvation Army Rest and play a few games of Ping-Pong. Each afternoon however, during the hottest part of the day, we reckoned to spend lying half-naked in our tents, either reading or sleeping – generally the latter. At teatime we would just have a cup of tea in camp and then, after a wash and brush up, go into the town to one of the hotels and have a real good meal.

Our favourite place was the Hotel de Poste which I had discovered on my day trip to Port Said earlier on. Here, for 12 piasters (2s 6d), a very good five-course, table d'hote dinner was served by native waiters dressed in long, white robes girdled with a broad, scarlet sash, in a large cool room refreshingly decorated.

These evening meals proved one of the most popular and enjoyable interludes of our whole leave. After dinner we would adjourn to one of the many French-style cafés and, sipping our cool Pilsner beer or port and lemonade, sit and watch Port Said go past. Sometimes we would go to the pictures but, as all the titles were in French and Arabic only, some of the pictures were not easy to follow. Needless to say, those ten days during which we lived and slept well and never went thirsty, passed all too quickly and we eventually left the town with very happy recollections of its hospitality.

Within a week of our return, the whole regiment was ordered back from Marakeb to El Arish, the journey down being carried out in easy stages with a night's rest at Rafah, Sheikh Zouwaid and El Burj.

Immediately on arrival at El Arish, an order was issued by the commanding officer that, in recognition of the recent hard work put in by the Hotchkiss gunners, they were all to have fourteen days leave at Port Said, quite irrespective of any other leave they may have had. Consequently, a couple of days later, I was again in Port Said with only 1½ piaster in my pocket, having drawn all my back pay on my previous leave.

However, I was not the only one, so, after borrowing sufficient cash, we had to cable home for a sub. We did this through Cook's travel agents and, as it happened to be on a Saturday, we got the cheap weekend rate. The cash was received on the following Tuesday.

Our time in Port Said was spent much in the same manner as previously, but this time a greater number of our own men were here with the result that, if anything, we spent a rather livelier time than previously. Then, a day or so before our leave expired, the Brigadier General, who was then in the town, came up to the camp to see how we were getting on and blessed if he didn't grant us all two more days' extension of leave!

Within the regiment, we gunners were inclined to be looked on somewhat as a nuisance, but it seemed that the 'heads' had a more kindly regard for us.

At any rate, those two extra days seemed to us the most enjoyable of the whole period.

On our arrival back at El Arish, we immediately found that routine had altered very considerably and that hard training was again the order of the day. During the next few weeks little spare time was granted to us. Tactical scheme training before breakfast almost every day, and saddles and equipment to be cleaned and polished almost to barrack-square standard, did not go down too well at this stage of our army career. Then we all had to go through a rifle firing course and the Hotchkiss gunners a further course of gun firing. Occasionally, when we had counted on a few hours free, we would be called out for remount riding or some other similar job. Consequently we were not at all sorry when early in September we started up the line again.

Before leaving, however, the men of our troop subscribed to purchase a cross which we got the Royal Engineers to make for us and which we erected in the little military cemetery to our late pal Jack Northover.

Our move carried us up almost to the Wadi Ghuzze again, at a point called Gamli. Since we last passed this place only a month or two back, it had grown almost out of recognition and was now quite a huge camp. We remained here for just over a month, but all our time was now spent on real active service work. Every morning, just before dawn, patrols were sent out across the wadi to points known as Rashid Bek, El Bugghar Ridge, point 630, and point 720, at each of which a strong outpost was posted and remained all day watching for any enemy movement. At night these posts were withdrawn onto the near bank of the wadi.

The Turks were doing exactly the same thing; the posts we used on their side of the wadi during the day were invariably occupied by them at night. Each morning a sharp little action ensued before they would give up the points of observation which we wanted. Point 720 was quite a long way out; from here it was possible to observe the Turkish cavalry patrols at work, but it was very necessary to be careful to prevent the post being surrounded.

During these days of late September and early October, troops, guns, ammunition and stores of all kinds were being brought up daily and massed at various points along the line. In the very air was a feeling that important events were afoot and each day this feeling became more intense until finally, on the evening of October 29th, we set off on what eventually proved to be the most glorious episode of the whole war in Egypt and Palestine.

13

THE FALL OF GAZA

— October 29th —

It was getting dusk when we started off. Crossing the wadi, we rode on all night away to the right flank. Just before dawn we found ourselves at Khalasa. Outposts were immediately sent out and, when it got light, we were able to see clearly the rugged hills surrounding Beersheba and to watch the operations of the enemy cavalry patrols. One patrol in particular we watched as it gradually approached our Hotchkiss gun post.

So well were we concealed that the patrol came within fifty or sixty yards of us without knowing we were there until we opened fire, at which they galloped off in a cloud of dust.

In the afternoon another squadron took over our outposts and, on rejoining the regiment, we were amazed to find the large number of troops – all cavalry – which were massed at this spot. We were given to understand that we – the cavalry – were to march during the night to the back of Beersheba, and so strike an unexpected blow at the strongly fortified Gaza-Beersheba line.

At midnight we moved off in one long column, four abreast, nearly five miles in length. What a ride it was too; thirty-four miles to cover, riding throughout the night like a phantom army, exact to time and on the very verge of the Turkish positions.

— October 31st —

By dawn we had done it and, when the sun rose, Beersheba was surrounded. At the appointed hour, the infantry attacked on their front and the Turks found themselves in a more or less helpless position. The Australians galloped in from the flank and, in a very short time, the town had been captured. There was, of course, the possibility of the enemy launching a counter-attack, so that we were kept in reserve just outside the town ready for any eventuality.

Nothing happened, however, until we were watering the horses at a well in a somewhat deep valley, when a number of enemy planes swooped down and gave us a pretty severe bombing. There being no means of escape we caught it rather badly.

Early next morning we rode through the town and patrolled amongst the rugged hills on the far side. In the afternoon we returned to Beersheba with the intention of spending the night there. During the night, however, the alarm was sounded and so, within a very short time, we were in the saddle again.

Riding during the remaining hours of darkness, and all the following morning, we approached fairly close to the Turks who were holding on grimly to some rugged hill country which contained several wells of water at a place called Khuweilfe. Concealing ourselves in a narrow wadi until it got dark, we then crept forward quite close to the enemy positions where, lying full length in an extended line, we kept watch on the enemy till just before dawn, when we crept back to our horses and again took cover in a small wadi. Of course, we were under fire most of this time, but fortunately most of the shells were passing over our heads.

During the morning we were ordered to leave the wadi, four men at a time, and gallop across a piece of open ground in full view of the enemy to a hill some five or six hundred yards away. After running the gauntlet through shell, machine gun and rifle fire, those who got there were immediately ordered to return, and so that very unhealthy piece of ground had to be crossed again. It seemed almost impossible for anyone to get safely through, but most of us did so.

An hour or so later we moved into a deep valley among the rugged hills in support to the Worcesters. It was something like thirty-six hours since we left Beersheba and our water had almost run out. As we were expecting to be relieved shortly by the Australians, most of us used up our last drop of water to make a billycan of tea.

Shortly after this we were preparing to retire when we were inadvertently bombed by one of our own planes. Almost immediately after, we were ordered forward again to reinforce the Worcesters who were being driven back. This meant a ride over a high rugged ridge and then down the forward slope in full view of the enemy. Machine guns, rifles and field guns were immediately turned on us and, before we reached the deep valley on the far side, many casualties had been inflicted.

Worse was to follow however, for just as the squadron reached the valley, a shrapnel shell burst just over our heads, causing great havoc. Dozens of men and horses went down in a trice, the wounded of both men and animals struggling in the dust and smoke. While the stretcher bearers darted about on their errands of mercy, the remainder of us went forward, dismounted with our guns, to a ridge in front overlooking the Turks.

As we went forward, I have a very vivid recollection of one episode. From out of the smoke and dust I saw one of my pals, Os Pallett, emerge and shout to me quite gleefully, 'I've got another one; in the arm this time!' and another Nuneaton pal, Bill Chamberlain, being carried away with several wounds in the chest. He was badly knocked about but eventually pulled through and returned in due course to the regiment.

The Turks were ultimately pushed back and we held on to our original positions until the Australians came up to relieve us. Then we immediately returned to Beersheba, arriving about midnight almost mad with thirst. Nearly forty-eight hours had elapsed since we started out with one bottle of water.

We now spent two or three days in Beersheba, before setting off again in pursuit of the Turks who were very strongly fortified at a place called Sheria. It was well into the night when we approached. At intervals we had rested for a few minutes at a time during our journey. Being tired, at most halts we were soon asleep after dismounting.

On one of these occasions, when we were roused by the order 'Get mounted', my mare was missing. The rest of the column moved on and there I was, left without a mount. Then I remembered that just before we halted we had crossed a shallow wadi in which there were small pools of water. I wondered whether my old mare had gone back for a drink. Walking back through the darkness and calling out her name, I eventually saw the dim outline of a horse coming towards me and, sure enough, it was my mare. I felt her muzzle and it was quite wet; she had found a drink. Being refreshed, we were able to canter on and soon rejoined the column.

As it got light, it soon became evident that the enemy was becoming demoralised and retreating hurriedly. Articles of clothing, equipment, clips of ammunition and personal belongings littered the line of retreat and we followed closely, on towards Gaza.

⟶ *November 8th* ⟵

This morning there was great cheering – Gaza had fallen at last! At this time we were about seven or eight miles from Gaza itself but well beyond the original Gaza-Beersheba line. The same afternoon, as we approached a small village called Huj, a battery of Turkish field guns and howitzers were holding up the advance of one of our infantry divisions.

At this point our Hotchkiss gun team, not having been able to water our horses for some considerable time (except my mare who had watered herself), were sent back a short distance to a wadi to find water for them. As we were returning to the regiment we heard a sudden burst of gun fire and, to our front, saw a cloud of dust rising. Then we learned that, so as not to delay the infantry advance any longer, two of our squadrons and one of the Worcesters had been ordered to charge the guns. Commanded by our colonel and led by our captain, Captain Valentine, the troops emerged from a small gulley in which they had been concealed and, forming columns of half-squadrons, charged straight for the guns. These were at once turned on them at point-blank range, killing men and horses before the shells burst. Most of the gunners stuck to their guns until they were sabred, while others rushed to man the machine guns which were mounted nearby. The charge, however, was pushed home with the capture of howitzers, field guns, machine guns and many prisoners, but at what a price? The scene during the next half hour was indescribable.

The prisoners were collected and set to dig one huge grave in which our dead were reverently buried together. Later on in the campaign, a wooden memorial, bearing a brass plate containing the somewhat lengthy list of names of the men who fell, was erected to their memory. It was estimated that our casualties amounted to nearly twenty-five per cent. As night came on, we bivouacked near the scene of this ghastly triumph.

Early next morning, a certain number of men were detailed to take the horses to water, each man riding one horse and leading two others. We were told that as we should not be away long, there was no need to saddle-up and that we could go in fatigue dress. Unfortunately, and to our dismay, we kept riding on from one point to another only to find that the well had run dry or that there was no well there at all.

This went on for hour after hour, first passing through cultivated plains and then high ranges of hills. None of us had any rations or water with us, and most were in shirt sleeves.

Naturally we were getting fed up; hope gave way to suspicion and despair, with the resultant groaning all along the column till, at about five in the evening, we came to a small Zionist village, on the outskirts of which water was being pumped from a well into a canvas trough. The water was only trickling through, and as it seemed that all the horses in Palestine had come to this one point for water, another hour or so elapsed before our watering operations were completed.

Having wandered about in all directions during the outward journey, we did not know exactly the distance back but, with sore seats after a day's bareback riding, we knew it was a lot farther than we cared for. Those who had tunics with them began to use them as saddles; but later on it became so cold that a sore seat was deemed preferable to a frozen spine.

Eventually we got back to Huj at about eight in the evening and were greeted with the news that the regiment was to be ready to move off again in an hour's time. So, by the time we'd had some grub and drawn our rations and feeds for the next day, it was time to saddle-up and away we went once more.

14

JERUSALEM

Following hard on the heels of the now-retreating enemy, we continually harassed them to keep them on the run and thus allow them no time to reorganise. Wherever possible they hung on grimly, especially at points of strategical importance, but we were constantly pushing forward.

Since our departure from Gamli, the regiment had suffered fairly heavy casualties, but our gun team still remained intact. By a strange coincidence, each of our five horses contained a figure 6 in its official number. The corporal's mare was No. 26; my mare was 56; No. 3's horse was 106; No. 4's horse was 86 and the packhorse No. 66. Not being sailors, we would not own to being superstitious, but this strange sequence of figures did give us confidence and we never feared going anywhere as long as we all went together. I point this out as a prelude to the episode which I am about to relate, and which, though it rather spoilt our sequence of numbers, still proved our amazing luck.

One morning, all the Hotchkiss gun teams were sent out under the command of our troop officer for the purpose of what was lightly called 'making a demonstration'. In other words, we were to persuade the enemy that, by engaging them at one point, the main attack was coming from there while, actually, the main attack was being launched at quite a different place. In this case, the main objective was an important railway junction.

Proceeding to the given point, it was not long before we came under shellfire. Dismounting at the foot of a fairly high ridge, several guns were at once taken forward and mounted on the ridge, immediately drawing heavy machine gun and rifle fire. While waiting for the order to get our gun into action, we sat in a small circle, we four members of the gun team and the officer's groom, each man holding the reins of his own horse.

By this time the enemy had got our range to a nicety and a shell exploded right in the middle of our little circle. When the smoke cleared, we found that the officer's groom had been wounded in the leg and No. 3's horse almost had its head severed – the rest of us were untouched.

At that moment, the officer came running down the slope, followed by the other gun teams, and ordered us all to get mounted and gallop back as quickly as possible. Here was a nice predicament: No. 3's horse was done for but we must get away or be captured. There was no time to argue, so the corporal got mounted and I legged up No. 3 behind him, while No. 4 galloped off with the packhorse. Mounting in quick time, I soon galloped off as well, with shells and bullets tearing up the dust all around.

By the time we reached the next ridge, in our immediate rear the Turks were in occupation of the ridge we had just left. Behind this second ridge we reformed while numerous riderless horses galloped about behind us. Our guns were mounted at intervals along this ridge and so kept the enemy occupied. At the first opportunity we rounded up one of the best-looking horses from those galloping about riderless to provide a remount for our No. 3.

Towards dusk we retired to a small village in our rear, where the rest of the regiment rejoined us and, in front of this village, we formed an extended line of outposts till morning. Several of these minor stunts and a continual harassing of the enemy carried us gradually forward until, towards the end of November, we had reached the foot of the Judean Hills.

The recognised wet season having now set in, we arrived at this point after a day and night of heavy rain, almost wet to the skin and with no prospect of getting dry. We were at the entrance to one of the narrow passes through the hills. With a constant stream of infantry artillery etc. going forward and a spasmodic stream of ambulances and Turkish prisoners coming in the opposite direction, we waited all day in the pouring rain for a chance to get through the narrow pass.

Eventually, at night, we bivouacked where we were – the place was called Latrone – and formed what shelter we could from the rain. By morning the rain had ceased and at last we moved on forward through the pass, which was still under shellfire, into the heart of that rugged range of hills which surround Jerusalem. At the top of the first steep ridge we turned off the road at a point called El Enab, and from here patrols and outposts were sent out into the surrounding wild hilly country. The post allotted to our squadron was in a little village about two miles away and perched at the top of a hill. To reach this we had to descend the rocky slope of a high ridge, leading our horses step by step, in single file, amongst the scattered boulders into a long deep valley. For a mile or so we were able to ride along the valley until we came to another very steep ridge running across our front.

Dismounting again, we had a very tortuous climb up the rocky slope to the village which was perched on its very summit. The post was mounted on the flat roof of one of the native houses and commanded a wonderful view of the enormous rugged hills and deep valleys for miles around. Shrapnel and high-explosive shells bursting over these hills and valleys echoed continuously.

Perched on another hill, some miles in front of us, was another little village said to be Bethlehem, but apart from that all we could see were hills and valleys. Each evening we returned to Enab where night posts were mounted. Every morning for just over a week we wended our way to the quaint little village on the hilltop, and each evening plodded our weary way back to Enab. Then, one morning, we returned through the narrow pass – with a sheer drop of several hundred feet on one side if one slipped over the edge – back to Latrone, where we had two days' rest.

— *November 29th* —

The whole regiment left Latrone this afternoon and, much to our surprise, found ourselves going down the line. All through the night we rode back through Junction Station and Ramleh, at each place finding that huge stores of forage and rations had been built up, together with a number of field hospitals.

Just before leaving Latrone we had received our first mail since leaving Gamli a month before, and how welcome were the smokes and other comforts we received, as almost everyone had run out of cigarettes long before this. For most of the night the column was wreathed in tobacco smoke issuing from a well-contented body of troops.

An hour or so before dawn we halted and bivouacked by the side of a small winding wadi where we could water the horses. Next morning, however, we started back up the line again, over the ground we had just covered in the opposite direction. After riding all day we reached the foot of the Judean hills again, just as it was getting dark. Sometimes walking, sometimes riding, often stumbling and generally grumbling, we struck off into the hills to the left of the pass at Latrone and continued until about midnight. Here we finally dismounted and, as it was impossible to get the horses any further, they were sent back. For the first time in our army career, we were left as glorified infantrymen.

When it eventually got light, we found ourselves in quite a deep valley, and all we could see was a high rocky slope in front of us, a similar one behind us and the sky overhead. With such a narrowed outlook, we remained in reserve and were given instruction in the art of bomb throwing. The following morning our gun team moved up the slope. Crawling over the top of the ridge, we mounted our gun on the far side, behind a barricade of rocks and boulders.

The ridge sloped steeply away from us into another deep, narrow valley, whose far side rose into a high rocky ridge similar to our own. This was held by the Turks who we could occasionally see moving about, and who continuously reminded us of their presence with bursts of rifle and machine gun fire and an occasional salvo from their field guns.

At night, a listening post was sent forward, almost into the valley, to give warning of any surprise attack which the Turks might attempt to launch, as they had apparently done on the night previous to our arrival. At that time, the Gloucesters were in our present position and, although taken somewhat by surprise, dozens of arms, legs and even heads protruding from little heaps of scooped-up earth all around indicated that the enemy had met with a very warm reception.

During our first day here it commenced to rain again and kept on incessantly, and with having no shelter but the rocks (our groundsheets had gone back with the horses), we were soon wet to the skin. However, a couple of days later, the Turks withdrew slightly and so we moved forward. From this position we could see Jaffa lying on the coast some miles to our left, and behind us, visible over the tops of the lower hill ranges, lay Ramleh and Ludd. Jerusalem, though hidden by the hills of Judea, lay on our right.

Still the rain came down. Up amongst these hills it was bitterly cold, and so, with merely a greatcoat and one blanket for protection, we huddled together behind rocks and boulders, wet to the skin. So sorry was our plight that bivouac sheets were eventually sent up to us and, with these, we managed to rig up some kind of shelter. Through such terrain it was impossible to bring any kind of wheeled transport, so our rations and water were brought up daily on camels, which invariably arrived with feet bleeding, torn and cut on the rocky ground which they had traversed. Thus rations were rather on the meagre side and water was brought up in just sufficient quantities for drinking purposes so that we could neither wash nor shave.

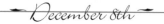

December 8th

Just a week after our entry into these hills, Jerusalem fell, causing the Turks immediately in front of us to fall back. We were now able to move forward into a small hill village called Shilta.

On the day we moved up, the rain eased and the welcome sun peeped out again. Needless to say we immediately set about drying out our clothes and, with water obtainable at a well in the village, were able to get a shave and wash and, incidentally, to carry out a bit of 'big-game hunting' in our shirts which, not having been removed for some weeks, were getting a bit lively.

In addition to sundry casualties received, the cold wet weather had laid several men low with pneumonia until, at the present time, there remained of our squadron (apart from the men who had gone back with the horses), an officer, two Hotchkiss gun teams and about six other men, including an RAMC orderly.

The two gun teams had to take it in turns to form a daily outpost on the ridge in front of the village from dawn till four o'clock in the afternoon. This was a rather risky job as it meant descending the steep ridge, on one side of which the village stood, crossing the valley at the bottom and then climbing the long, steep boulder-ridden ridge in front. Carrying the gun, spare parts and ammunition, in addition to our own equipment, this trek was in itself hard enough but, at the end, just we three men with a gun, out of sight of the rest of the squadron and, on account of the rocky ground, were unable to see very far either to the right or left. In case of attack it would have taken the best part of an hour to get back to the village.

The slope, on the far side of the valley in front of us, was sparsely covered with fig and olive trees, around which herbage of some kind grew. All we saw on our first day on this job was a shepherd bringing his flock to feed on what herbage there was. He remained there all day, tending his flock.

On alternate days, when we remained at Shilta, we were engaged in building a strong barricade all around the village, which meant that our party got little rest. This went on for about a fortnight until a few days before Christmas we were relieved by a regiment of Australians and returned to the ridge that we had previously occupied in front of El Burj. Here we erected our bivouac sheets between the rocks and only just in time, for on Christmas Eve it came on to rain again and continued right through Christmas and Boxing Day. During these days we sat huddled in our low shelters talking of previous Christmases and, although the only Christmas fare we received was an issue of red wine and the usual rum issue, we were cheerful enough to make the hills ring with carols inspired by the happenings which they themselves had witnessed. Our repertoire was not confined solely to carols, however; it ranged from 'Perfect Day', through 'Mademoiselle from Armentières' down to 'If the Sergeant's Pinched Your Rum Never Mind'.

15

FAREWELL TO THE HORSES

— 27th December —

Just before dawn, we moved along in support of the infantry who were launching an attack along the line on our right. The attack being successful, we retired in the afternoon and bivouacked in one of the deep valleys a short distance in our rear.

— December 28th —

A party of us were sent out with picks and shovels for road making. This was a hard job, removing rock boulders of all sizes and shapes and blasting through rock barriers, and thus smoothing out, as far as possible, a track for the camels to travel along with the rations.

The next day, we went on along the valley continuing our road making operations, and so on for the next two days. This brought us up to the last day of 1917 when, at two in the afternoon, we were relieved and marched back over hill and dale down to El Burj, where we had left our horses on December 1st.

During the night the rain started again and New Year's Day dawned with the rain pelting down in true Palestinian fashion. However, during the morning, the horses were brought up to us and that was sufficient to dispel any heaviness of heart which the climate could inflict on us. Never had a saddle seemed so comfortable, or the motion of a horse's tread so soothing as on that morning when, in the pouring rain, we rode out of the hills back to Latrone having – although unaware of the fact at the time – fought our last fight in Palestine.

The almost incessant rains of the past month had absolutely saturated the low lying ground at Latrone; water oozed up at every step and the horse lines were soon churned up into a sea of soft, slimy mud. Still the rain pelted down and, as darkness came on, it became obvious that the ground was far too wet for us to lie down to sleep. We lit a fire and organised several parties to raid a nearby forage dump for sufficient wood to keep the fire going all night. Throughout the night we sat on empty biscuit tins and chunks of wood in a large circle round the blazing fire, singing songs and, at intervals, making hot drinks of tea, cocoa and Oxo.

Towards dawn, the rain ceased and, after the usual breakfast of bread and bully beef, we saddled up and started off down the line. Passing through Ludd, we headed for the sand dunes which fringed the coast, striking these at Yebna in the late afternoon. There on the sand we spent a comfortable night and rested during the following day and night.

— January 4th —

We spent another day in the saddle, riding back as far as Esdud, which is the 'Ashdod' of the Old Testament. Here we spent one night, continuing our journey the next day as far as El Medjil and here, during the night, the rain came again.

— January 6th (Sunday) —

We continued through the pouring rain as far as Giza where, on the outskirts of the town, we bivouacked on solid ground again. I say solid, although it was almost like mire. When we woke up next morning we found ourselves lying in puddles of water with blankets and clothes saturated. However, we were soon on the move again, covering the final part of the journey to Belah. On arrival here we were mighty pleased to find that our camp was to be pitched on the sand about half a mile from the sea. Horse lines were laid and tents erected so that we were under cover again.

During the first few days there were, as usual, endless jobs and fatigues to keep us busy. This was the first time since we left Gamli in October that we had been really out of range of the enemy guns and, having come back so far, we knew that we were likely to remain here for a few weeks at least.

On the day after our arrival we received our Christmas mail and there is no need to say what rejoicing this caused. During the early part of our stay here we were not worked too hard; the horses were exercised each morning, saddlery and equipment were straightened out and cleaned and deficiencies replaced.

There were however two very tiresome fatigues which came round all too quickly. The first of these was ration fatigue, for which a party of men from each troop was detailed each day. Proceeding to the huge forage dump, enclosed with barbed wire, this party had to carry the rations and forage for the whole mounted division, carrying the various items outside the compound and arranging them in dumps ready for the transport of each respective regiment to carry away. As this entailed lugging something like forty bales of tibbin, thirty or forty sacks of barley, and a like number of sacks of other forage, numerous cases of jam, bully beef, biscuits, condensed milk, sacks of sugar, bread, dried fruit and umpteen cheeses, it will be readily realised how popular this fatigue was, representing, as it did, some four or five hours' work.

The other 'popular' job was the pumping fatigue. The whole camp drew its drinking water from a large well just outside the village of Belah. The water was pumped by means of an apparatus used by the natives but, whereas they employed a couple of blindfolded oxen to keep the machinery working, the British Army, thinking more of its horses than of its men, made the latter perform the part of the oxen.

The apparatus consisted of two huge wooden cogwheels some ten feet in diameter, one arranged horizontally and the other vertically so that the cogs fitted into each other. Round the vertical wheel ran an endless chain carrying dozens of small metal cups. From the centre of the horizontal wheel protruded a long shaft of wood. As this shaft was pushed or drawn round the well, so the cogwheels were set in motion. The endless chain of cups descended into the water, coming up full, then passed over the top of the wheel where they were automatically tipped upside down. The water fell into a trough and then into a huge canvas tank erected by the Royal Engineers. Here, of course, the water was sterilised before use.

As some of the cogs on the wheels were broken, some of the cups missing and others leaking, it was a painfully long job going round and round in circles until the tank was full.

~ January 19th ~

As it had been impossible to celebrate Christmas in the usual festive manner, it was arranged that the Christmas feast should be held now; so all the men sat down in the open to a real, good meal provided by the officers, and at which the officers and NCOs waited on us. This act was appreciated by us all and was typical of the happy relations which had developed between all ranks during the past two years of service. The dinner was followed by a concert which, like the meal, was thoroughly enjoyed.

The following day – a Sunday – the whole brigade attended a funeral service held in memory of the many comrades who had set out with us to Beersheba but had been left sleeping in various corners of Palestine.

On the Monday we were inspected by the Corps Commander – General Cheval, an Australian – and on Tuesday went over to Belah station for another of those fumigation episodes previously described.

Now there is no end to the trades which the British Tommy is expected to be able to turn his hands, but surely there can be few stranger than the one with which a party of us were occupied during the next few days – brick making!

About a mile from camp there was a large pool of water, from the edge of which we had to dig out the mud, put it into moulds and then leave the brick-shaped lumps to bake in the sun. I would not like to describe the bricks which our earliest efforts produced, but before long we were able to turn out the stuff true to pattern. These bricks were being used to build a bathhouse for the troops, but which we were destined never to use.

In the middle of the camp a pitch was prepared where both football and rugger were played, and everyone was encouraged to take part in these games. The football, as usual, held a strange fascination for me and very few afternoons passed without my taking part in a game of some kind, either for the troop, squadron or – the highest honour of all – the regiment.

The regimental games were played against other regiments lying anywhere between Belah and Gaza, so that some of these away games provided nice little outings for the players.

With the arrival of February, our routine became more serious and strenuous again. Every morning we had mounted drill or tactical schemes and, each afternoon, Hotchkiss gun drill followed by a saddle or arms inspection.

— February 11th —

We commenced rehearsals for an inspection by General Allenby. We would all have been most delighted to parade for the general, who, during the last operations we had so often seen right up at the front directing operations himself, but we did not relish the extra work of polishing up saddlery and equipment and rehearsing ceremonial drills etc. which such an occasion made necessary. However, a few days later we were informed that the parade had been postponed indefinitely; in fact, it never did take place.

— February 27th —

Towards the end of the month, leave was granted and, having the opportunity of going with the first party, I grabbed it and arrived in Port Said for the third time.

Having had very few pay days since October, my pay book showed quite a handsome credit balance, out of which I was able to supply myself with quite a few little luxuries during my ten days' leave. However, as I have previously described a typical holiday here, and as this was spent in typical manner, there is no need to give a further description of the happenings. If anything, this leave was even more enjoyable than the previous ones for, after passing through the many perils and hardships of the past few months, it was real enjoyment to visit and welcome again the sights and places having some resemblance to civilian life. The same ladies serving refreshments at the Empire Club, the same genial 'missionary' at the Salvation Army Rest and the same old De Lesseps at the entrance to the canal, all helped to convey a sense of stability which had certainly been non-existent during the preceding months.

— March 10th (Sunday) —

We arrived back at Belah and were soon informed by our pals that the brigade was going from bad to worse in the matter of red tape and poshness. Soon after our arrival in Egypt we had been referred to as 'The Immaculate Warwicks' in one of the English papers. However, having during the past two years, been a part of the Australian Mounted Division, we soon wiped out all chance of again being described as 'immaculate', to such an extent that the Divisional General had once declared that we were the most ragtime crowd under his command. But now it seemed that we were again in danger and all because the Duke of Connaught, representing the king, was coming out to inspect us.

With spit, polish and burnish we worked on our saddlery and equipment and in the end to no purpose for, after being twice postponed, the inspection never took place at all.

— March 16th —

Sports and recreation were still in progress, but the star turn was a race meeting to be held at the 'Red House' – a landmark well known to all troops who had taken part in the Gaza operations. Unfortunately, the day turned out wet but, in spite of this, troops from all over the place rolled up, some on foot, others on horses and even some on camels. Much excitement prevailed and, as one of our own officers won the big race of the day, celebrations were called for.

During the next few weeks, parties were sent out each day on salvage work to the positions around Gaza. Each party was allocated a certain section in which they had to dismantle the barbed wire, collect ammunition etc. – in fact, anything that could be salvaged from the Gaza defences.

— March 31st (Easter Sunday) —

Just before Easter – always a momentous period where our regiment was concerned – various rumours circulated round, some to the effect that we were soon going up the line again, and others that we were going to Italy.

The whole regiment was ordered to parade dismounted; the Divisional General rode up and calmly informed us that the remainder of the brigade were ordered up the line again, but we – the Warwicks – were going to France and, after wishing us the best of luck, rode off.

Our brigadier, with whom the Warwicks had always been popular, then made a little farewell speech in the course of which he emphasised the fact that our transference to France had been conferred on the regiment as an honour, each brigade having had to nominate its best regiment; the 5th Mounted Brigade had nominated the Warwicks. We, however, did not regard this move as any honour!

April 1st

The rest of the brigade moved up the line again and we all paraded to bid them farewell. On the Wednesday we handed in our cavalry equipment – swords, spurs, revolvers and saddles, after which we organised a burial service in front of the officers' lines, in which a pair of spurs were more or less reverently consigned to the earth and a wooden cross erected with an appropriate inscription.

But the saddest moment of all came next day when we had to part with our horses. That was indeed the unkindest cut of all, for during the period in which the regiment had made some sort of a name as a fighting force, we realised that the horses had been as important as the men and, intelligent animals as they were, appeared to be proud of the regiment to which they belonged.

On the following day – Friday – we were issued with shrapnel helmets and sun helmets. On the Saturday we handed in the Hotchkiss guns, with very little regret, and were now issued with gas helmets.

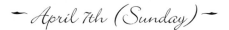

April 7th (Sunday)

We paraded and marched as infantry to Belah Station, where, to the accompaniment of music supplied by the band of the Yeomanry Division, we entrained – thirty-eight men per truck – to the tune of 'Good Bye', and bade farewell to the horses and Palestine.

16

HORSE TALES

Here it might be appropriate to digress somewhat and explain some of the characteristics of some of the horses which we had just left behind, and also some of the reptiles and insects which we had encountered.

First the horses: As in the case of humans, there are hardly any two horses exactly alike in shape and size and temperament. Our gun team packhorse was quite a character on its own; a sturdy Australian animal with only one eye – how it came to lose the other we never knew – which we named 'Cobber'. We all carried a sand muzzle, strapped around the horse's neck when not in use, and it was the stable guard's duty to put this on the horses when they had finished feeding, to prevent them grovelling in the sand. Old Cobber had the knack of getting his muzzle off, chewing through his head rope and making off to any forage dump he could find. On many occasions we had to search the horse lines of the whole brigade for our missing animal who, on some occasions, was absent for several days on end.

Of course, all the horses were branded with their regimental initials and squadron letter, so that the truant was always ultimately returned. My own mare was quite well-behaved on the horse lines and very seldom broke loose. On the march we carried a nosebag of feed on each side of our saddle and, after roughly each hour's ride, we would halt and dismount for ten minutes' rest. This was when things happened, for she had a habit of getting her teeth into the nosebag on the saddle of the next horse to her and, in a jiffy, tear a hole in it so that the contents trickled out for her to eat. Not at all a popular action in the eyes of my 'next-door neighbour', so I had to carry a piece of string or an old bootlace with me to effect emergency repairs on these occasions.

Some horses were terrified of camels and my mare never took very kindly to them. If we were out on duty at night time I could always tell if any camels were in the vicinity as she would prick up her ears, turn her head in their direction and break out in a sweat.

Other horses had their own peculiarities, such as blowing their stomach out on being saddled up so that the girth could not be properly tightened, and others give one a playful nip in the pants when being groomed, but there were very few real rogues.

Amongst the pests native to the country, I think the worst was the camel tick. A small, black, crab-like creature which infested the camels and horses by crawling up the leg of the animal and, finding a part where the skin was thinnest, sucking the blood – a most loathsome creature.

The two most dangerous pests, as far as humans were concerned, were the tarantula spider and the scorpion. The tarantula is somewhat attractive looking in quite gay colours, but with a poisonous sting or bite. The scorpion is another crab-like creature in shape, but larger and of a different colour to the camel tick. It has the sting in its tail which it rapidly darts over its head while still facing its prey. We did, at times, gain some sort of amusement by catching a tarantula spider and a scorpion and putting them face-to-face in a box or tin to make them fight each other.

There were, of course, lizards of all sizes and colours which were quite harmless but quite interesting to watch as they darted among the rocks or boulders. The chameleon was a most attractive little reptile and a great fly catcher. When in camp we liked to get a chameleon in the tent to watch the fly-catching, or to put it on the outside of the canvas and watch it change colour as it crept over the camouflage.

Then there was the large black dung beetle – quite harmless, but always busy like the ants. In that hot climate the horse dung soon dried into small lumps and these beetles used to work hard in pushing a lump at a time to a hole which they would make in the sand, just as the ants work on a smaller scale. When on outpost duty, to while away the time, we used to mark a circle in the sand, divide it into four quarters and in the centre place one of these beetles on its back and bet on which section of the circle it would be in when it got on its legs again.

Apart from the creatures mentioned, the flies, of course, were always with us and in some parts of the country mosquitoes were rather troublesome, but there was nothing else of special interest.

17

ALEXANDRIA

Being packed too tightly to even sit down, let alone lie down, we lolled on our kits singing songs and telling yarns while the train dragged us across the southern part of Palestine and the Sinai desert to Khantara, where we arrived about half past seven the next morning.

Khantara, we found, had completely changed from the small sleepy place we had known in the spring of 1916 to a huge base bustling with activity, with new roads, great forage and ration dumps, base hospitals and recreation huts for the troops. In the evening we crossed, once again, and for the last time, the pontoon bridge over the Suez where two years previously I had been on police duty.

At Khantara West we eventually boarded a train of open trucks which chugged its way through the night to Alexandria where we arrived about the middle of the morning next day.

We must have looked like a regiment of chimney sweeps, for the smoke and dirt from the engine had given us a nice thick coating of black. Once off the train, we immediately proceeded by tram to Sidi-Bishr, one of the seaside suburbs of the city. Here we were allotted tents already pitched on the beach.

At five in the evening we were all granted a pass till midnight and there were very few men who failed to explore Alexandria that night. Knowing our ultimate destination, and naturally assuming that we should soon be crossing the Mediterranean again, everyone drew their back pay and set about making the most of the time while it lasted.

Every morning we had to spend a certain time at manual and physical drills, and then attend a compulsory bathing parade. That brought us up to dinner time and, apart from picquets and camp guards, ended our day's work.

After the first day, passes were granted from four o'clock in the afternoon, which left a nice long time to spend 'downtown'. While the cash held out, most of that time was spent in eating and drinking and attending various shows. Each night, for the first week or so, three or four of us would go to one of the hotels and have a four- or five-course dinner and a bottle of wine. Then, after a sightseeing stroll through the more noted streets, such as Boulevard Ramleh, Rue Marseilles and Rue Cleopatra, adjourn to one of the many taverns which displayed such titles as 'English Bar',' Café d'Allies', 'Hotel de France' etc. and, over a bottle of beer and peanuts, talk of the past and offer opinions regarding the future.

Occasionally we would visit the casino or 'Cinema Gaiete', at each of which a musical hall performance was given and to which there was no charge for admission; the price was put on the drinks.

On the Saturday after our arrival I was detailed for picquet, and the particular picquet to which I was attached, consisting of eight men under a military policeman, was detailed for the beat in 'Rue des Soeours', known to all servicemen as 'Sister Street'. This was a narrow winding street, if it may be called a street, in the dirtiest and lowest part of the city. From seven o'clock in the evening till half past ten, we had to patrol through this quarter imbibing the sickening stenches which emanated from the filthy little shanties that lined both sides of the thoroughfare. In this neighbourhood, brawls and even riots were not uncommon, but fortunately, on this occasion, nothing untoward took place.

On the following afternoon – Sunday – several of us walked out to Nouzha Gardens, which is Alexandria's most beautiful park. A band was playing and the Alexandria locals were strolling about with their heavily veiled girlfriends.

In the evening, Frank Carter and I adjourned to an Italian restaurant called 'The Star of Italy'. Here, servicemen were specially catered for with very reasonable prices; a good meal of three or four courses cost only 5 piasters (just over 1s), and a bottle of burgundy, 6 piasters (1s 3d). Naturally, it was always well patronised by troops of various nationalities and, on that account, the strange but rather enchanting atmosphere, at once apparent in the civilian restaurants, was lacking, but a rapidly shortening purse made accommodation more important than atmosphere.

— April 19th —

The end of the week and we had another pay day, after which we were able to again partake of an evening meal at one of the more expensive restaurants and also to pay an occasional visit to one of the several cinemas in the town.

All this time, with no definite news of embarkation, we were having a most enjoyable time thinking little of the morrow until we were nearly all broke and, knowing that many of us had overdrawn our credit, there was little to look forward to.

One evening, four of us met in the town and, pooling our money, managed to rake together 5 or 6 piasters. We figured that this would just about buy us a glass of lemonade and a cheap cake each (what a fall from four-course dinners and wine!). We entered a small tea shop and, after trying unsuccessfully to diddle the proprietor, we spent quite a long time over a glass of lemonade and a very small cake.

Such was our present financial position that we decided we would all look through our kit and anything we could in any way call 'superfluous', we would try and sell to a native in the town next evening. Consequently, on the following evening, armed with a razor, jackknife and one or two other similar articles, we made our way along some of the darker side streets in an effort to raise the wind with these possessions. After much bartering, we eventually made a few piasters; enough to take us to the little lemonade and cake shop again.

— *April 29th* —

Machine gun classes were started. For this purpose we were divided up into small parties, each under an instructor, and given instruction on the weapon which we were to use in France – the Vickers machine gun. Those of us who had been Hotchkiss gunners soon picked up the intricacies of this new weapon, although the gun itself was quite different in principle and action, but more about that later.

— *May 3rd* —

Another pay day rolled round and so things were quite bright again ... for a time. By the time of the next pay day, the quartermaster had apparently found time to check up on each man's pay book, with the result that instead of the 100 piasters for which I had indented, all I got was the equivalent of 4s, and some men received less than that.

Consequently, instead of the nightly trip into Alexandria, which necessitated a train ride each way, one or two of us began to substitute a country walk to a little native village called Bacos, where there was one small café where monkey nuts were given out free with the beer. Very few troops were encountered here, which suited us fine, as we could not afford to sink all our pay at the present rate in one round of drinks.

Alexandria itself, at least the modern part of it, was quite like a European city and many Europeans reside in its several beautiful suburbs. At one of these, Bulkeley, which lies between Sidi-Bishr and Alexandria proper, there was a little English church at which troops were always made welcome. Quite a few of us attended the evening service most Sundays, although we could not help the 'church expenses' to a greater extent than half a piaster.

18

THE SINKING OF
THE *LEASOWE CASTLE*

On the Wednesday following my 4s pay day, embarkation orders were issued and we handed in our kitbags to be transported to the docks. On the following morning we were conveyed by train from Sidi Bishr to the docks, and stepped straight aboard the troopship *Leasowe Castle* just after midday.

On the Friday, we drew away from the quay into the centre of the harbour, from which position we could see several other transports already loaded with troops, and others still loading up at the various quays.

May 26th (Sunday)

After remaining all day at anchor the previous day, at eight o'clock in the morning we were issued with lifebelts and given instruction on how to use them. Furthermore, each unit was allotted an emergency station at which to parade immediately once an alarm was sounded. Just after three o'clock in the afternoon we began to move from our moorings and soon joined quite a procession of transports which formed our convoy. This comprised the *Kaisar-i-Hind* (the flagship), the *Malwa*, *Indarra*, *Caledonia*, *Canberra* and our own ship.

On reaching the open sea, a 'W' formation was adopted with an advance screen of destroyers, one of which was flying a large sausage-shaped observation balloon. Further destroyers, sloops and submarine chasers formed a bodyguard all around us and we all felt well protected. (During the past few months, many troopships had been torpedoed in the region we had to traverse, hence this formidable looking escort.)

Remaining on deck until land was out of sight, by which time the novelty of watching our mighty escort had worn off, we went down below for tea. However, it was very hot and stuffy down here and the vibrations from the ship's engines made the deck a much pleasanter place. Furthermore, smoking was not permitted below deck and up above no smoking or lights were permitted after dark. Consequently, the last hour or so before dark found practically every man on deck puffing at his pipe or fag as if his very life depended on it.

Darkness crept on until the order was given, 'All pipes out', by which time we could just discern the outline of the ships on both side of us and, occasionally, the very dim outline of one of the escorting destroyers. Bringing our blankets on deck (most of us preferred to sleep on deck at our emergency station), we sat in little clusters chatting and joking. By the time we got into our blankets, the moon had risen enabling us to see more clearly the other ships again. Nuneaton was well represented in our little cluster on deck, for Bill Chamberlain and myself were lying side-by-side on the deck, and Os Pallett was swinging from a hammock which he had slung on two hooks over our heads. With his feet dangling over the side of his hammock and gazing up at the moon, he rounded off our conversation by jokingly repeating the caption from one of Bruce Bairnsfather's cartoons: 'This blinkin' moon will be the death of us.' Little did he know how prophetic his words were.

I don't know exactly how long I had been asleep when I was awakened by a terrific explosion. Jumping straight out of my blankets, I ran to the side of the ship and looked overboard. There was the sound of hissing steam and our propellers whizzing round out of the water. I could not, or would not, believe that the worst had happened until, in the fitful moonlight, I was astounded to see the other ships racing ahead of us. Then I realised it was not they who were travelling faster, but us who had stopped.

From the deck above, orders were being shouted and there was a scurrying of feet; they were lowering the lifeboats. On our deck we put on our lifebelts and, as soon as the sergeant arrived, we paraded in the usual manner while he called the roll. Then we waited patiently, watching the packed lifeboats pulling away and a destroyer steaming round and round at full speed, enclosing us in a dense screen of smoke.

There were no lifeboats anywhere near our station, and so we still stood there, on parade, until our squadron officer came along and quietly said, 'Well boys, you can see the position; there are no more lifeboats or rafts, so you had better jump overboard and trust to being picked up later.'

By this time the ship was beginning to settle with her back well down and the bow and stern rising higher and higher out of the water. So we proceeded to go overboard and poor old Chamberlain, who could not swim, hesitated and asked my advice. I advised him to follow me, as he would have a better chance by doing that, than by remaining on board. There was a rope hanging over the side of the ship which I descended, but found that it did not reach nearly to the water. It was a sickening feeling when I had to release my grip on the rope and drop into the water below.

In the darkness I did not see another soul, although there must have been hundreds of others in the water. I struck out strongly to get as far away from the ship as I possibly could before she sunk. After a time I turned on my back to see how far I had gone, but did not seem to have made much progress. Striking out again, I swam and swam until I was thoroughly exhausted and now just floated about almost aimlessly.

It is impossible to describe my feelings when, at last, I heard singing and in the distance discerned the dark outline of a lifeboat whose occupants were singing, 'Swim Sam swim, and show them you're some swimmer.'

I tried to shout but could not raise a sound, so I started splashing my hands on the water, and someone shouted, 'Where are you? We can't see you.'

Again I tried to shout but no sound came and so I again started splashing my hands on the water. The boat drew nearer and then I heard a voice say, 'Be careful you don't hit him on the head with your oars.'

At last the boat came within reach and I madly clutched its side, but was too weak to pull myself up. Willing arms shot out and dragged me in, head first, and there I lay for some time with my head in the bottom of the boat and my feet on the seat at the side.

Very soon I was sick, bringing up some of the salt water which I had swallowed. Then I began to feel better and, sitting up, could hear members of the crew giving orders to each other and, on looking round, found that we were heading for a sloop which was standing by to pick up survivors.

Barging through a crowd of empty lifeboats which were floating about the sides of the sloop, a rush was made to grab a rope hanging over the sloop's side near the bows. In single file, we commenced to climb this rope and, just as I was doing so, the moon peeped out from the clouds and by its light I saw in bold letters the name of the ship – *The Lily*. At the sight of this English name I immediately felt safe again and was soon on board.

Immediately after, there was a loud clatter, a hissing of steam, a muffled report and we saw the poor old *Leasowe Castle* break in two and slither below the water. I was cold and began to look for shelter, eventually deciding that the warmest place would be near one of the ship's funnels. There I squatted with my back against the funnel till it got light next morning. Of course, I was wet through and my sole attire consisted of a shirt, tunic and lifebelt. I could feel the ship was moving but in what direction I had no idea.

When it got light I began to look around to try and find anyone I knew, and soon came across one of our officers who asked me whether I had seen the colonel or the adjutant, but I had not. It turned out that they had both gone down with the *Leasowe Castle*. I then came across one of my pals of the old Hotchkiss gun team, lying in a corner with his face cut and swollen almost out of recognition, the result of a blow from an oar of one of the lifeboats. I went in search of a MO to dress his wounds and make him as comfortable as possible.

On the upper deck I came across a party of men from my own troop and, by degrees, others came along and so we all remained together. So far we had had nothing to eat, drink or smoke since the previous evening, but we were just thankful to be alive.

By this time the sun was very strong, and what clothes we were wearing soon dried out. We tried to dry out any tobacco or cigarettes we could muster, but this was not at all successful.

About midday a large tin of bully beef and biscuits were brought up and placed in the middle of the deck for us to help ourselves. Unfortunately, the metal plates, of which the deck was composed, were so hot by now, that blistered feet were risked in the inevitable barefoot rush to the bully tin.

By this time, we had almost reached the minefield which lay outside the harbour of Alexandria, and half an hour later land became visible. At about two o'clock we entered the harbour where ambulances and a stack of clothing were waiting to greet us. We could not travel through the town in just our shirts, and so we were immediately issued with a pair of shorts and a sun helmet, and were provided with tea and rum, after which we were conveyed by train back to our old camp at Sidi Bishr. Here a meal was soon provided, but the attendance was very small; barely a third of our squadron being present. Most of my particular pals were absent – Frank Carter, Os Pallett and Bill Chamberlain – but we learnt that other ships had gone out to pick up survivors and no doubt many of the present absentees would turn up later.

Fortunately, many of them did turn up during the night, including my three pals, but nearly 200 men lost their lives, including our colonel and adjutant.

19

ACROSS ITALY BY TRAIN

In spite of the recent tragedy, much laughter was provoked at roll call next morning by the motley crowd which assembled. Some appeared in naval caps and army slacks, others in sun helmets, no shirt but baggy naval trousers, and some in just pants, socks and a knotted handkerchief on their head.

During the morning we were issued with necessary kit to the extent of knife, fork and spoon, and later on with shaving tackle. The following day we were each paid an Egyptian pound (100 piasters) which at first we took to be a gift, but found later that it was deducted from our pay.

A memorial service was held in memory of the men who had been drowned. The same evening many of us attended evening service at the little English church at Bulkely. In fact, so many men turned up that two services had to be held, a practice which was continued during the remainder of our stay here.

It took some considerable time to completely re-equip us all, and weeks passed by before we again received embarkation orders.

Reveille was at half past three in the morning, and after breakfast we left camp at quarter past five to entrain.

After a somewhat slow journey to the docks, we went aboard the troopship *Caledonia* at about eleven o'clock in the morning, but remained in harbour until half past one in the afternoon the following day. Then, with a similar escort as before, the convoy again passed out to sea.

The terrors of the previous voyage meant everyone wished to sleep on deck, instead of down below. In the ordinary way very few men would think of bringing their blankets up on deck till just before dark, but on this, our first day out at sea, every available inch of deck space had been booked by tea time. Consequently there was no alternative but for many of us to sleep below. Our mess deck was the second one down from our emergency station, which meant in the event of any emergency having to make one's way up two companion ways, most likely in darkness. I therefore slept right at the foot of the lower companionway, determined that if anybody had to get out it was going to be me!

At this time, the sea was somewhat choppy but by the next day, which passed by uneventfully, it became much calmer, and by the afternoon of the following day, it was as calm as a lake. To see such a vast expanse of water with hardly a ripple was somewhat weird.

June 21st

At half eleven the alarm was sounded and everyone raced to their boat stations. The escorting destroyers could be seen darting about at full speed and, at intervals, great columns of water spurted up, denoting the explosions of depth charges. All lifeboats were slung out ready for launching and we were kept at our stations for an hour and a half, but nothing serious happened and we were given the welcome order to 'Stand down'.

Land was now faintly visible, and in the late afternoon we entered the outer harbour of Taranto. Passing slowly through the very narrow entrance to the inner harbour, we finally anchored in midstream and were then taken ashore in lighters. It was a great relief to be safely across that dangerous stretch of water and be on land again, at last – streets of gold could not have been more welcome to our feet than the rather dirty banks of Taranto's inner harbour. Adjoining the harbour was a large rest camp composed of wooden army huts in which we were billeted.

Mail was awaiting us on arrival – the first we had received since about the middle of March over three months ago – so there was quite a large accumulation of men. One thing that seemed very strange to us was the long period of daylight. In Egypt there had been practically no twilight darkness immediately following the setting sun, but here it was light up to ten o'clock at night.

After a peaceful night's sleep followed by a hearty breakfast, a further batch of mail arrived, so now we were well supplied with news from home and many little comforts, including tobacco and cigarettes. The remainder of the morning was spent in loading rations onto a train; a train that was apparently to take us on to France.

At ten to three in the afternoon we entrained; thirty-two men were loaded into each truck and, as we were aware that the journey would last for several days, we resented this sardine packing and were not slow at voicing our grievances, but all to no avail. At last the train started and our final view of Taranto through the open door of the truck was of the good old *Caledonia*, lying peacefully at anchor in the quiet harbour.

Our first stop was at Brindisi, which lies on the Adriatic coast of Italy, and here we drew a mug of tea. We had already realised that there would not be sufficient room on the floor of the truck for us all to lie down to sleep, so here at Brindisi we pinched one of the seats from the platform and lifted it into the truck. This, at any rate, would accommodate two men lying down, or four or five sitting up.

The train moved on again, and after making a supper of the rations which had been issued to us, the two sliding doors of the truck were closed; candles were lit and stuck on mess-tins or tin hats or anything else handy as we prepared to get down for the night. It was a tight squeeze, but with two men on the seat and the remainder on the floor we just about managed it.

The train did not stop again until about midday the following day at Foggia, where another platform seat found its way into our truck. Tea and rations were issued and we were allowed to have a wash. Then off we went again; the extra seat provided slightly more sleeping room and we settled down to sleep that night more comfortably than on the previous one. No sooner had this happened than the train pulled up and, after a short time, we opened one of the truck doors to hear the shout, 'Tea up!'

Needless to say we were very soon out of our blankets and dashing up the line to get our mugs filled. This was at about ten o'clock at night and our next stop was at half past six the next morning at Ancona, where we were provided with cups of coffee by the American Red Cross. Later on in the morning we stayed for an hour at Faenza, where rations were issued and we were able to have a wash and shave. The same afternoon we reached Bologna where we had tea, after which we travelled on without another stop until dawn next day. We were now at Voghera, where tea was once again served out to us.

The journey was now beginning to tell its own tale in the health of the troops, due to the conditions we had to endure. At almost every stop, men were reporting sick and soon the hospital van attached to the train was full, and sick men were now being left at hospitals all along the line. Several 'casualties' had occurred in our truck, which, at any rate, left more room for the survivors.

Just after midday we arrived at Genoa, where tea and rations were again issued, and then on to Savona, which we reached during the evening. We were now almost on the borders of France, and at dawn next day we found ourselves passing through the Riviera; San Remo, Monaco and Cannes were names we were able to note as we passed through.

At about nine in the morning we pulled up at quite a small place, of which I was unable to ascertain the name, and here we had our usual breakfast of tea and bully beef. After this we travelled on for many hours without a stop and, as this was our fifth day on the train, we were all getting pretty fed up. Eventually we pulled up at Le Teil, where tea and rations were once more issued. Later we passed through Lyons without stopping, but stayed for a short time at some other small place, apparently without a name, followed by another night in the train and then a short stay for breakfast at Malesherbes. Then on again through Versailles to a place called 'Us' where tea was served. Then followed another night of torture, but happily the last, for at ten to eight the next morning – June 29th – we arrived at Étaples which was our destination.

Having left Taranto on June 22nd, we had spent a good week on the train and, out of the men who originally occupied our truck, not more than half arrived at Étaples.

20

THE WESTERN FRONT

We were soon marched to a rest camp near the station, where all the tents were sandbagged and camouflaged and numerous little trenches could be seen all over the camp. Apparently this place was almost a nightly target for German bombers and our first night here proved no exception.

The second night they came in relays and kept up the bombing from ten to eleven in the evening till half past one in the morning, during which period we remained huddled up in the open trenches. So this was France!

However, on that day, the first man from the regiment had proceeded on leave to England and, although it would take some considerable time at the rate of one man per day, it was sufficient to revive our dwindling hopes of seeing Blighty once again after nearly three years.

July 1st

We were issued with an extra blanket and new shrapnel helmets. Having decided from the experiences of the previous two nights that night-time in camp was not at all healthy, the third night saw several of us take our blankets and groundsheets into a wood outside the camp to sleep. The enemy planes came over as usual but no bombs were dropped near the wood.

July 3rd

We moved into a training camp a mile or so out of the town, which was situated in a fairly thick wood bordering on the road to Camiers. The other side of the wood was bounded by the railway line which ran to Boulogne. The only drawback to this camp was that on the opposite side of the road lay the gas school where cylinders of gas were stored. One bomb on that would have gassed the whole of Étaples. It was not surprising then that we were at once issued with the latest type of gas helmet.

Our move to this camp signalled the official ending of the Warwickshire Yeomanry. From our regiment and the South Nott's Hussars, who had also come with us from Egypt, one composite battalion was formed and given the official name of the 100th Battalion Machine Gun Corps. All surplus men, including my old pal Os Pallett, were sent over to England. Although most of them hated to leave the old regiment, the thought of getting back to England sweetened the pill somewhat.

From this point onwards, until we finally went up the line some six weeks later, practically the whole of our time was taken up with machine gun drill. Divided up into sections with an NCO from the Life Guards as our instructor, we spent seven hours a day at gun drill and it soon became apparent that the instruction we had received at Alexandria was only a very small part of what we must ultimately learn. During those long and tedious days of instruction, every little detail was drilled into us to such an extent that it seemed impossible that we should ever forget them.

The Vickers Light Automatic, to give the gun its official name, was composed of two parts: the tripod which weighed 48lbs and the gun itself, which as far as I can remember weighed 28lbs. However, as the gun was water cooled, this added another 10lbs to its operative weight. The gun was fed with ordinary rifle ammunition from canvas belts each holding 350 rounds and was capable of firing a belt at the rate of almost 1,000 rounds per minute.

The somewhat intricate mechanism was very wonderful, yet the actual principles quite simple. When a round was fired, the force of the explosion drove the moving parts forward. The power of recoil was supplied by the resultant escaping gases, assisted by a spring on the side of the gun called the fusee spring. So thoroughly did we have to learn every little detail that, finally, we not only had to dismantle and reassemble the gun blindfolded, but also to carry on at any stage at which another man left off.

All this took several weeks to digest, and a further week to learn the stoppages, before we came to the actual firing. We would have to wait until July 20th before we had our first firing practice, and that was only short-range.

— July 30th —

A concert party of WAAC's (Women's Auxiliary Army Corps) were good enough to come and give a concert in the gas school just opposite the camp. Almost the last item on the programme was a parody of one of the then-popular songs, which was composed apparently by the singer herself. It more or less depicted army life in Étaples and the chorus started off, 'I've a sneaky feeling around my heart that something's coming down.'

No sooner had she finished than something was coming down, in the shape of bombs from enemy aircraft.

About a week later another concert was given, this time by Lena Ashwell's concert party, composed mostly of professionals. It was by far the best concert we had heard all through our army life. The song 'Roses of Picardy' was encored umpteen times and, during the following months, was echoed from trenches and dugouts scores of times by members of our battalion.

August 1st

We were taken to the machine gun range at Camiers where we had to fire a full course at all ranges, and this was again repeated about a fortnight later.

There now remained but one more item to learn, though it was perhaps the most important and in many ways the most complicated. This was barrage firing, for at this stage of the war, machine guns were being used chiefly for barrage firing in conjunction with the artillery. In such cases it was indirect firing. The actual target not being visible, it was worked out from a map and the gun positioned on the target by compass. This was just about the last item in our gun training which had occupied our first six weeks in France.

Other items entered into the general routine as well, such as infantry drill (not at all popular with us), gas drill, camp guards and, most Sunday mornings, a march to Étaples for a hot shower/bath.

Occasionally we would take an evening stroll into Étaples or Camiers, and at one of the local estaminets partake of *vin blanc*, which was reasonably cheap and more palatable than French beer.

August 16th

This day was a particularly happy day for me, for my name was read out on the leave list at last, though I knew it would be a week or two before I actually got away. Unfortunately this happy day was followed by instruction in infantry equipment which we had never worn before. Instruction in assembling the belt and braces, valise packing and other important details made us suspicious that it would not be long before we were sent up the line; this time it was to be the line of the British Expeditionary Force, with trench warfare in place of the open spaces we had been used to in Egypt and Palestine.

August 25th (Sunday)

So it came about that on this day, instead of going on leave to Blighty, the whole battalion entrained at half past four in the afternoon for an unknown destination, 'somewhere in France'.

Having been loaded into trucks similar to those in which we had travelled from Taranto, we soon passed through Abbeville, ultimately arriving, after a journey of some six hours, at Longueau, just outside of Amiens.

It took some time to unload the limbers in which the guns and ammunition were carried, and it was nearly midnight before we started off on our first route march. Fortunately it was dark so that we could see little of the damage and desolation wrought by the earlier fighting, but the distant horizon was alight with gun flashes and the occasional star shell.

After marching for about four hours we arrived, just before dawn, with blistered and aching feet and sore shoulders at a badly battered village named Pont-Noyelles. We were billeted in a roofless and windowless house whose floors were strewn with broken glass and plaster, but on which we were glad enough to lie down and sleep. A few hours of sleep were enough to somewhat revive our drooping spirits and, after an early morning wash at the village pump followed by a hasty breakfast, we were soon on quite good terms with ourselves again.

At half past eleven in the morning, with packs and equipment readjusted (our march of the previous night had taught us more than any previous instruction), we started off again. Along the straight and mostly tree-lined roads of France we marched, passing at various points derelict lorries, guns and GS Wagons. Stumps of trees in the midst of large areas of shell holes bore testimony to the ugly work that had been in progress.

A march of two hours or so brought us to the small town of Franvillers, where we were billeted in a large barn at the back of a house still bearing its number – 73 – and in a street at the corner of which its name still stood – Pond St. We remained here for two days.

— *August 28th* —

At about one o'clock in the afternoon, we marched on again some miles to another small town called Warloy-Baillon. We were now within sound of the guns, although only an occasional long-distance shell dropped in the town. Our billet was a large wooden shed on the outskirts of the town, a hundred yards or so from a line of trenches and redoubts, which at some time had been the front.

On returning to our billet the following day, after a route march and gun training, I was warned for leave to England for September 15th. Another happy day, but again marred by an enemy air raid in which bombs were dropped so close to our billet that I had doubts as to whether any of us would see September 15th.

Further disappointment was to follow however, for next morning it was read out on orders that all leave had been cancelled.

— September 4th —

We marched out of Warloy-Baillon on the next step of our journey to the front. Passing through Albert, we were brought face-to-face with the grim realities of war on the Western Front. Shells had now fortunately ceased to fall on this unhappy town which had changed hands several times, but not before it had been reduced to a town of brick dust. The streets, such as they were, lay inches deep in red brick dust as they threaded their shell-pitted course through heaps of bricks and broken furniture. Here and there a gaunt wall, once the side of a happy homestead, held a shattered picture and, in some cases where part of the floor remained, it supported a dusty piano or an armchair. A twisted mass of metal and woodwork overhanging a street had once been a railway bridge over which the trains had passed to the fair-sized station, which was now almost impossible to identify.

We simply passed on through this stricken and deserted town, on through the monotonous French highways to Trônes Wood, thus completing a march of some fifteen miles.

Trônes Wood existed in name only now, for a few short tree stumps were all that remained of the wood itself, its shell-pocked face and a number of plain wooden crosses indicating the cause of its obliteration.

After a night's rest in the open, we moved on a further nine miles to a spot south of Combles, where we remained temporarily in reserve. Two days later we moved forward again, to a quarry near Nurlin. We were now within shell range, almost in-line with our own observation balloons, which could be seen floating about like huge sausages at various points along the line. Here we were billeted in tunnels at the bottom of the quarry, where we were comparatively safe.

Soon after our arrival, the first and second sections were sent up into the line, but I was in the third section – so far so good. Two days later, these two sections returned, but the fourth section was sent forward and I was sent with them to complete one of the teams not at full strength.

Starting off at dusk we soon had to cross a main road which was being heavily shelled, and then across what had once been an open field. Beyond this we went on to a narrow lane, which we followed for some distance until we passed a battery of our own artillery that was sending shells over to the Germans pretty quickly.

We stopped here for a short time and, having got over our reintroduction to shellfire – we had not been under fire since the previous December 31st – soon became sophisticated British Tommies once more and the usual banter and jesting began to flow.

As an enemy shell would come sizzling towards us, someone would shout, 'Keep low boys and trust in Beechams,' and, after the explosion, a remark to the effect that it would give one a nasty headache if it hit them upstairs.

Our machine guns were now unloaded from the limbers, and we proceeded along another narrow lane until we came to a communication trench, along which we advanced in single file. Rifle and machine gun bullets began to ping over our heads and zip into the sides of the trench which, we were glad to find, got gradually deeper and deeper. After twisting and turning for some time, we reached what we took to be the front line trench. Of course it was quite dark and we tripped over duckboards and slipped into muddy holes before arrival at our allotted station.

The guns were immediately mounted and, from the fire step, we took our first peep over the parapet into no-man's-land which, apart from spasmodic bursts of machine gun and rifle fire, lay strangely quiet and still.

With the guns mounted, one man from each team was posted as sentry for two hours at a time, while the remainder crept into the improvised dugouts to sleep.

Pride mingled with anxiety is the most apt expression I can find to describe my feelings as I stood on the fire step that night, with eyes strained across that strip of ground which lay between the Germans and me: proud to feel that I was at last in the very front with England and the whole British Army behind me, but anxious to know what would happen if the Germans suddenly launched an attack against us who were strangers to trench warfare and, at the moment, were holding this part of the line in very small numbers.

Shells of various sizes were constantly passing over, with an occasional one or two dangerously close to the trench. An occasional star shell lit up the ground in front, showing Jerry's wire entanglements and shell holes of all sizes. Those two hours on the fire step, seemingly eternal, at last came to an end and, once rolled up in my blanket, I was soon asleep.

21

LEAVE

Fortunately, my first spell in the trenches was of short duration for, on the following night, we were relieved and went back to the spot where we had left the gun-limbers on our way up; this was on the outskirts of Guyencourt. Apparently, however, we had only moved back in support to another unit, for we remained here on open ground with no protection from the shells which constantly burst around us all through the night.

September 16th

The rest of the company came up and so I rejoined my own section. That night, under cover of darkness, the whole company moved up into a very shallow trench to the right of the spot where I had been previously. All through the night we dug away deepening the trench, making a good parapet, gun emplacements and dugouts. Just before dawn we left off digging and were given a rum issue. Throughout the day we rested and then, again at night, dug our trench still deeper. The guns were then laid for firing a barrage. Reveille was to be at quarter to five the next morning.

Lying or lolling in the dugouts to snatch a few hours' kip before zero hour, we were soon aroused with the shout, 'Gas over!'

Hastily donning our gas masks, we waited for the atmosphere to clear and eventually receive the all clear sign. Again we dozed off to sleep, and again came the shout, 'Gas over!'

We were now cursing the Germans for so upsetting our slumbers, but gas is gas and we soon put on our masks again. In fact, many of us fell off to sleep still wearing them.

When zero hour arrived it was pouring with rain and still dark. Then our artillery started all along the line and we joined in firing at our nominated, but unseen, target. For an hour and a half the deafening blitz went on, as though the earth was being torn up and flung in huge chunks at the Boche. The enemy replied with counter-fire but, judging from the stuff that was going over from our lines, one would expect the Germans' front line to be pretty well slaughtered.

At a given signal the firing stopped and the infantry came up from behind us and went over the top. Through the pouring rain in the grey semi-daylight, they went forward but, after only a few minutes, many of them ran back to take cover in our trench, saying that a German tank was advancing straight at our position. The tank immediately came into view and we trained our gun on it but, as it got nearer, a Union Flag was displayed and it turned out to be one of our tanks which had lost its way.

We now dismantled the guns and followed up the infantry as far as a sunken road. After waiting here for a time, we moved across to the left into a trench in front of Épehy. This trench was almost knee-deep in water with duckboards floating about in it, and, as it turned out, this was to be our 'home' for several days.

Fortunately the rain now ceased, and after patching up the tattered parts of the trench and erecting gun emplacements, the guns were mounted and pointed at Épehy (which, at the moment, was in no-man's-land).

Both German and British shells could be seen bursting in the town and, after dark, flames lit up the ruins of what had once been Épehy. We remained here for four days until the night of September 21st, when we moved about half a mile into a drier and better-constructed trench. Leave was now again renewed and I knew my turn must be pretty close.

— September 22nd (Sunday) —

After another rain-filled night, rations were brought up under cover of darkness, when four men from each section were detailed to go to a certain point about half a mile away to draw them. On this particular night I was one of the ration party. We got safely to the appointed spot and duly loaded ourselves up with the issued rations. On the return journey we had to cross a stretch of open ground before we reached the trenches.

While we had been drawing rations we could hear an aeroplane buzzing about overhead but, as that was nothing unusual, we took little notice of it. However, just as we were crossing the open piece of ground, a battery of our own artillery passed us and immediately a bomb crashed almost at our feet. We were all flung to the ground and in quick succession four or five more bombs fell almost simultaneously, smothering us with lumps of earth and mud as we lay flat on our stomachs. It was a terrible few seconds but not one of us was hit, even though the bombs dropped all around us.

After that we got back to the trenches as quickly as our legs would carry us.

— September 23rd —

I was detailed for leave to England. Leave men were supposed to draw twenty-four hours rations before leaving the line, but the rations did not come up till after dark. The Germans were well aware of this and they invariably put up a nightly 'strafe'. As there was a good mile of open ground to negotiate before reaching Company Headquarters, and having now been in the army long enough to learn how to scrounge a few rations if necessary, as soon as it began to get dark I said goodbye to the lads and started off on my journey. As it was, I had to dodge a few shells and, by the time I reached headquarters at Guyencourt, they were falling thick and heavy.

I immediately sought the officer's cook who I knew well, and he soon served me up with a meal with as much tea and rum as I liked, and then fixed me up with a wire-netting bed in the corner of his little kitchen next to the fireplace. I was soon very comfortable, with the only disturbing element being the shells bursting outside. To me they were more disturbing than usual at the moment, for having come so far safely, it would have been very unlucky to get hit when actually on the way home. However, I was soon asleep.

When I woke up next morning it was broad daylight. After a good breakfast with more tea and rum, I set off at ten in the morning on the next step of my journey, this time to Battle Headquarters, which were situated close to the quarry at Nurlin.

Proceeding at a good pace so as to get out of shell range as soon as possible, I had nearly reached my destination when I discovered I had left my greatcoat at Company Headquarters. I quickly decided that I would not go back for it on any account, but try and borrow one.

I remembered that one of my pals was with Company Details at the quarry, so I headed straight there to find him, and he immediately let me have his coat. Then I raked out a signaller I knew and got him to send a message to Company Headquarters to ask them to send my coat to the quarry by the first messenger.

At Battalion Headquarters I joined forces with the men from the other companies of the battalion who were going on leave – four of us in all. We were issued with a clean change of underclothing and then sent into an outhouse to have a bath, with instructions to report later for our pass and final instructions.

Eventually, at about four o'clock in the afternoon, we were ready with our passes in our pockets and instructions to board any lorry going down the line until we reached a light railway which ran beside the road. Carrying out these instructions, we arrived at Péronne at about half past six and were put in a rest camp under canvas with scores of other leave men from various units.

At six-thirty the next morning we marched through Péronne to Le Catelet, where we boarded a train and, after a journey of nearly eleven hours, eventually arrived in Boulogne, where we spent the night in barracks.

Next morning, we marched to the docks and went aboard at about half past ten, ultimately disembarking at Folkestone at about one-thirty in the afternoon. A long train was ready waiting; a real passenger train, too – this must be England! Kindly officials guided us, allotting so many men to each compartment.

Arriving at Victoria at about five o'clock in the evening, we were guided to the pay office where we handed in our pay books and received £2 on account, with an assurance that the remainder of our back pay would be forwarded to us in about two days.

From this point we went in different directions. After waiting nearly two hours for the train at Euston station I eventually arrived home at twenty past eleven in the evening on Thursday, September 26th, having spent over three days travelling.

Little need be said of the next fourteen days or so, as that is already family history, but the worst day – or rather night – was on Tuesday, October 15th, when I finally left home to catch the 2.30 morning train.

I was soon back in London; on to Folkestone and straight off the train and onto the boat. By midday I was back in Boulogne. This was considerably quicker than the homeward journey had been, but I had already made up my mind to lose as much time as possible in getting back to the battalion.

22

ARMISTICE

On disembarking we were all marched up to Ostrohove No. 5 Rest Camp and allotted tents where we were to spend the night. Early next morning we had to parade and, according to the division to which we belonged, were instructed which train to catch and at what point to alight. Our battalion now ranked as corps troops; that is to say, we were sent to any division in the corps that needed temporary machine gun support, and we were often attached to two and even three different divisions in one day.

I reported that I was unaware of which division I belonged to and had no idea of what part of the line the battalion now occupied. I was therefore ordered to remain in camp while the necessary enquiries were made, and thus spent one day here. Unfortunately, by next morning the officials had ascertained the location of the battalion, and I was ordered to take a train to Roisel.

Leaving camp at six o'clock in the morning, in company with two or three other men in a similar position to myself, we spent all day in the train. It was dark and pouring with rain when we reached Roisel. Here, after a night in the rest camp, we were issued with rations next morning and ordered to parade. An NCO gave us a rough idea of where the battalion was stationed and said there were two ways of getting there; one was to march there under the command of an NCO, the other was to 'lorry jump it'. Needless to say we all chose the latter.

Our little party, now three in number, decided that once on the road we would take our time and walk all the way instead of lorry jumping, and thus waste another day or two. By midday we were tired, hungry and thirsty and so, climbing a low wall surrounding a little battered churchyard, we sat down and made a meal of bully and biscuits.

After this short rest, walking seemed more of an effort than ever but, sticking to our resolutions, we trudged on. At the end of another hour or so we took another rest and more refreshment, after which our once-strong resolutions began to waver. However, we took to the road again and trudged on for some time until, running short of water and rations, we held a little council, at which it was unanimously agreed that we should board the next lorry that came along in our direction. Within an hour or two of this I was back at Company Headquarters at Premont, the company itself being in the line in front of Reumont.

I spent the night and following day in quite a comfortable billet, but at dusk I was ordered up the line with a party of other details. A march of some four or five miles brought us to the village of Reumont, where we joined the company who had just come out of the line. Many familiar faces were missing and there were sad reports of the casualties which the company had suffered during my leave.

— *October 20th* —

After spending the night in a dilapidated house, with shells falling all around, the whole company returned on this morning to Premont.

— *October 22nd* —

We marched up the line again, this time as far as Le Cateau. Under cover of darkness, we proceeded through the town on to the rising ground beyond. Here, in dead silence, each gun team dug themselves in, forming a deep emplacement of a crescent shape for each gun.

Just as we were completing the work, the Germans apparently got wind of our presence and set up a very fierce bombardment which they kept up all night. This was absolutely the worst night's shelling I ever experienced. The enemy had our range to a nicety and pumped shells of all sizes into us all through the night. Crouched down in the bottom of our little crescent-shaped trench, whose sides shook with the vibration of the bombardment, we remained silent, expecting every moment to be blown to pieces.

At a certain hour we had to fire a barrage in conjunction with the artillery, after which the infantry went over and apparently captured the enemy positions without much trouble – when it got light, there was no sign of our infantry in front of us, nor of any Germans.

By this time all firing had ceased and, before long, we strolled across to the German trenches, finding that they were not more than 200 yards in front of us. Had we been aware of the close proximity of the enemy during the previous night we should not have had such easy minds during the digging operations. The enemy front line trench was almost full of dead Germans and, beyond this, numerous wounded were lying about, having apparently been hit while trying to get away.

Towards midday we moved back to Le Cateau, which was still being heavily shelled. Here we were billeted in quite a large house in what appeared to be the main street of the town. Although the house had been somewhat shattered by shellfire and was almost windowless, it was quite comfortable as compared with the trenches. We remained here for nearly a fortnight. Just previous to this, however, the battalion transport was short of men, owing to so many being on leave, and I volunteered to join them. For several days, our section sergeant would not let me go, but later the position became so acute that he had to let me go.

— *November 1st* —

I went over to the transport section, which was billeted in another part of the town. I say 'billeted', although this meant sleeping under the limbers in an open field. However, I had a horse again, in fact two horses, for I was assigned to take over the leading pair of horses in a GS Wagon.

— *November 4th* —

We moved up to Pommereuil, but apparently the Germans were now on the retreat, with the result that next day we moved on to Landrecies. We remained standing to arms here for two days, during which it rained the whole time. We were provided with shelter in a large barn, outside the door of which lay a dead German; apparently killed as he was attempting to get away.

— *November 7th* —

Late in the afternoon we moved on to Noyelles again, where we spent the night. It was still pouring with rain, and horses and mules are not the nicest of things to be looked after in such weather, especially at night. However, there was no more foot slogging for me, and so I was quite prepared to take the rough with the smooth.

Early next morning we moved on to Dompierre, where the transport remained while the company went into the line. We remained here until Sunday, November 10th, when we moved on to Bas-Lieu, close to Avesnelles, still in pursuit of the Germans. The rain had now ceased and it became very cold. During our night here, where we slept in an open field, there was a sharp frost but next morning it was fine and bright with sunshine.

As we harnessed up, there were rumours of an armistice but, as no official news was forthcoming, we assumed that these rumours, like many others which had been current, were without foundation. However, as we entered the next village, we found flags flying from almost every house and the villagers ran out of doors and cheered as we passed by. We now began to think there must be some truth in the rumours and, when we finally halted at a village called Les Fontaines, where the transport was left under the temporary command of the quartermaster sergeant, he informed us that the armistice had actually been signed.

To us the news sounded too good to be true and was hard to believe. However, we were soon fixed up with billets in a large room behind a small cottage, whose occupier informed us that the Germans had only left there a few hours earlier. As I was able to speak a little French, I had to act as interpreter and learned that the cottage was occupied by this man, his wife and mother-in-law; the two women being in bed seriously ill. He was so delighted to see us that he would have given us anything and thoroughly cleaned out our billet before he would let us enter, as he said it was not fit for us after the 'dirty German pigs' had been in it.

Needless to say it did not take us long to make ourselves comfortable in our new billet, and our rather meagre rations were supplemented by vegetables from our 'landlord's' garden, including haricot beans which he had successfully hidden from his late tenants.

He took me in to see his wife and mother-in-law, to show me how ill they were, after which I explained the situation to our quartermaster sergeant and cadged a few issues of rum for the sick people. Unfortunately we did not remain here long enough to observe the effects of the medicine for, on the following afternoon, we were ordered to pack up and move forward to join the company who were at Sivry, a large village several miles away.

We were now in Belgium, not far from Mons which, since the early days of the war, had been well behind the fighting zone. Consequently the towns and villages bore few marks of violence and the shops and estaminets, carrying very limited stocks, were at least open for business, which enabled us to lead a slightly more civilised life than we had for some considerable time past.

During the week we spent here, we were ordered to clean and polish all our harness and equipment as it was likely that we were to go right on into Germany to form part of the Army of Occupation. Naturally this did not go down very well with us; the war was over and all we wanted to know was how soon we were going to get home. The fighting was definitely over, which somewhat lightened our hearts, even if the wait for demobilisation was going to be a tedious one.

After a week at Sivry, where we were comfortably billeted opposite an estaminet which we often visited, we moved on to a muddy little village called Jamoille, spending one night at Froidchapelle on the way.

— November 24th —

On Sunday, November 24th we moved forward again to a fair-sized place called Rosee. Here we were billeted in an empty chateau standing in its own large grounds and, although the large bare rooms were rather cold, with many having stone floors, we were able to make ourselves fairly comfortable.

On the Friday following our arrival, the transport wagon in which I rode the leading pair of horses (and which actually belonged to the Army Service Corps) was ordered to be returned to the ASC. We were instructed to take this wagon to a town called Morialme, which lay eight or nine miles away, where we should join up with wagons which were being returned by other units. All the other drivers were ASC men and were consequently returning to their own unit.

Arriving at Morialme in the late afternoon, we found one or two wagons already there, and in a short time others rolled up. Then a sergeant major, already half drunk, rode up and took charge of the assembled convoy. Having parked the wagon with the others and tethered and fed the horses, I considered my job was over and, being anxious to get back to the battalion, with hope of an early demob, I informed the sergeant major that I was immediately returning to my own unit. He, having already found an estaminet close at hand, was by now properly drunk and, in language which only sergeant majors can use, told me that I was going on to Charleroi with the rest of them next morning, asking who was going to look after my two horses if I didn't?

Beyond telling him that it was his funeral not mine, in his present state I could see it was useless to argue further, so I went to the billet we had been allotted in a little tumbledown cottage, quite certain of the fact that no sergeant major would see me in Charleroi.

In the billet I handed over my two nosebags to the other man on my wagon and told him that before dawn next morning I should be up and away, without saying a word to anyone, and make my way back to my own unit.

By the time it got light next morning, I was well on the way back to Rosee. I had a few rations with me which I ate as I tramped along, and by the middle of the morning I had reached Florennes. I found a café where, over a cup of coffee and some cakes, I rested for half an hour or so before taking to the road again. Eventually I arrived back at Rosee at about two in the afternoon, tired but quite happy.

One morning, the transport officer called the corporal and myself and suggested we went and inspected an abandoned German wagon down the road, which appeared to be in serviceable condition. If it was useable then it would be handy for doing odd jobs and, when on the move, for transporting the officers' kit. Everything seemed to be in order, so we hitched it to a pair of horses and I was appointed to drive the wagon back to our lines and thereafter to take charge of it.

A few days later, I was told by the transport officer to get the wagon ready for two o'clock to take another officer and himself to Florennes, where they were going to spend a few hours. With the corporal as escort on his own horse, we duly arrived at our destination where the officers left us, saying we could unharness and tie up the horses but be ready to start back in about two hours' time.

The corporal and I wandered about the town for a while, spent half an hour or more over a cup of tea and cakes at the café which I had previously visited, and then got ready for the return journey at the appointed time.

My old section was holding a celebration dinner that evening and had invited me to join them. Two suckling pigs had been purchased and were to be specially cooked for the occasion. The two officers, however, were so late in returning to the rendezvous that I was in great fear of being too late for the feast, but just made it in time. What an enjoyable feast it was too, with ample portions of everything that was going and French wine worthy of the occasion.

December 14th

We left Rosee and, after spending one night at Dinant, went on to Ciney, which was quite a large town compared with most other places we had stayed. I was now travelling in comfort, seated on the box of the German wagon and able to wrap myself up with a groundsheet or blanket in the cold weather.

At Ciney we were fixed up with billets, fully expecting to remain until after Christmas. Ciney was a typical Belgian town with its cobbled roads and footpaths, but it also contained a good range of shops and estaminets where it was possible to purchase most of the commodities which come within the range of a soldier's pay.

23

THE FINAL MATCH

The war had now been over for more than a month and we could not be persuaded to take any real interest in harness polishing, equipment cleaning and the 'posh' parades which general officers are always so fond of holding when there is no actual fighting in progress. At any rate, it was said to be as a form of punishment for parading slovenly that, on the fourth day after our arrival at Ciney, we were taken away from the comforts of town life and stuck in a little village called Seringchamps, where we were billeted in the harness rooms and outhouses of a large chateau, while the officers occupied the chateau itself. However, with the thoughts of demob in our minds, coupled with the fact that Battalion Headquarters was four or five kilometres away in a village called Haversin, we did not mind much.

Football teams were now being organised and one morning I was given instructions to drive over to Ciney to collect a set of goalposts which had been ordered from the local wheelwright there. It was a bright and frosty morning when, escorted by the corporal on his horse as usual, we set off with the German wagon to Ciney and, after an hour or so, pulled up at an estaminet for a rum and cognac. At Ciney, the goalposts were not quite ready and so we left the wagon and horses there while we strolled through the town and bought ourselves a few items of food.

On our return to the wheelwrights, the goalposts were already loaded up on the wagon, but the crossbars were of such a length that the forward ends protruded beyond my seat on the box. However, all went well on the return journey until we came to descend a long, steep, but fortunately straight, hill. Here I applied the brakes but, apparently, the weight on the wagon was too much for them to hold, and the wagon began to gain speed quicker than the horses until it touched their hind legs at which they broke into a gallop. The wagon was now swaying violently from side to side, with the ends of the crossbars threatening to knock me off the seat with every swing. I managed to hang on till we reached the level ground again, where the corporal caught me up and said he nearly fell off his horse with laughter. He had never seen anything so funny in all his life as the wagon and horses careering down that hill, with the wagon swinging from side to side and me desperately hanging on. He had the fun, not me.

We then proceeded slowly, until we found an old boot which we nailed on to the brake block in case of further need but, as usual, we eventually delivered our cargo safely.

When the football got into full swing, each section formed a team with Transport and Company Headquarters staff combining. At this, my old section wanted me to return to them, but the transport officer and the company sergeant major wanted me to stay and captain their side. I was on the point of deciding to return to my section when the officer called me to see him and said if I would stay he would offer me the easiest job in the whole battalion. On enquiring what this would be, he said I was to be his groom. As he only had one horse and already had a groom, I asked what my duties would be and he replied, 'Play football.'

That settled it. I stayed on and we had some enjoyable games between the various sections. I was then selected to play for the company in a match at Battalion Headquarters. Our transport officer, with the idea of showing the headquarters staff that even if they had consigned us to a remote country village we could still do things in style, got out a stage coach that was housed at the chateau, and the harness for four horses.

Selecting the best four horses we had, we gave them a short rehearsal on the day before the match, and everything seemed satisfactory. On the great day the team and as many supporters as the coach would carry gaily took their seats and, to the merry tootle of the coaching horn, proudly trotted out of the village.

It was a lovely day (after many wet ones) and we were quite enjoying our ride, until descending a long steep hill with a sharp turn at the bottom. This hill led into the village of our adversaries. Down this tree-lined slope we began to gain speed, until we were going too fast to be comfortable. The driver was turning on the brake without any apparent effect and, in an effort to steady the now galloping horses, gave one final sharp turn at the break wheel, lost his balance and fell overboard, with the result that the horses simply bolted.

With the trees flying past us at a seemingly amazing speed, there was nothing for it but to jump clear of the coach. Like most of the others, I landed safely in the ditch at the side of the road and, on climbing out, saw the poor old coach leaning on its side at the bottom of the hill with the horses facing in the opposite direction to which we had been going.

A broken harness, which we were able to repair, and a splintered spoke or two in the wheels was the extent of the damage, and so, after all, we drove on to the ground in great style, no one but ourselves knowing what had happened.

Although the coach waited to take us back again after the match, not one of us would risk it, preferring to walk the four miles or so back to Seringchamps.

Christmas Day passed, with the exception of mail from England, very much as any other day, on fairly short rations. The excuse given was that the civil population had to be fed for the time being.

For some days there had been no butter issue so, being able to speak a bit of French, I visited several nearby farmhouses, with the officer's official groom as companion, to try and buy some butter. They all said no to my enquiries, but at one place the daughter of the owner opened the door and, after my enquiry, held a short conversation with someone inside who I could not see. Then she explained that they had no butter for sale but that we could go in and help ourselves to bread and butter and coffee at a table where the farmhands were doing likewise. This was very welcome and we were invited to go again, any afternoon, and sit down with the farmhands that came in from the fields at about half past three to four in the afternoon. We repeated the visit several times.

Apart from giving the officer's groom an occasional hand with his horse, I had little else to do apart from play football. Most mornings the groom and I would take a stroll in and around the village, calling in at one of the estaminets for a cup of coffee. At one of these I enquired whether there was anybody in the village who would do a bit of washing for us, as our shirts, socks etc. had only had a dab-wash in cold water for some considerable time. The lady herself said she would do it for us and so, one morning a week, we took round our laundry and a few days later called again to collect it.

This set up quite a laundry trade in the village for, as soon as other men heard of it, they all wanted the same service.

New Year's Day arrived and life still went on in the same easy but, at times, monotonous manner, until a few days later the first batch of men left for demobilisation.

― *January 7th* ―

I received my declaration from the Advisory Committee stating that employment was waiting for me. The filling up of the necessary forms was followed by a wait of nearly a fortnight until, on Sunday, January 19th, I was instructed to be ready to proceed for demobilisation on the following Wednesday.

The next day it was rumoured that demob had been stopped and on Tuesday this was officially confirmed. At this there was much grumbling and grousing but, in the main, life went on in the same monotonous manner as during the past month or so. It seemed that it was going to be a much harder job to get out of the army than it was to get in!

On Friday, January 24th, I was called on to sign further forms, and was mighty glad to be informed that demob was to recommence on Sunday and that I was to leave with the first party.

— January 26th (Sunday) —

Having bid farewell to our remaining pals, at eight o'clock in the morning our little party marched gaily along the avenue which ran past the chateau and, with no regrets at all, turned our backs for the last time on Seringchamps.

At Battalion Headquarters a lorry was waiting to take us to Andenne, where it had been snowing. Andenne was one of the Belgian towns which had witnessed some of the worst German atrocities in the early days of the war. In a small café, where I enquired for a cup of coffee, the proprietor and his wife, both prematurely white-haired and utterly broken in spirit, told me of some of the terrible happenings. In the shops were displayed picture postcards and actual photographs of some of these atrocities.

After spending the night in this town, we entrained at half past ten the following morning and, although the journey to Dunkirk took nearly thirty-five hours – two days and one night – it seemed nothing, for every minute thus spent meant another minute nearer England.

Arriving at Dunkirk at about half nine in the evening on the Tuesday, we spent the night in the arrival camp and, after a compulsory shower/bath the next morning, proceeded to Mardyck Departure Camp. Here we were put under canvas, which was not at all pleasant in the bitterly cold weather and with snow on the ground. We remained throughout Wednesday and Thursday until, on Friday morning at about half past nine, we were marched to the quay and, after a long wait there, eventually boarded the SS *Scotia* about midday.

It was still bitterly cold and so, without troubling about a last glimpse of Belgium or France, most of our little party went below. Putting our kit and equipment on the floor, we made ourselves as comfortable as possible. There we remained singing, joking, smoking and dozing until we reached Dover just as it was getting dark. Consequently we did not stand, as so many fictional heroes do, with eyes strained on the white cliffs of Dover, watching them come nearer and nearer. As a matter of fact, we didn't much care whether the cliffs of Dover were white or black, as long as there was a gangway from the ship to allow us to step once again into England.

Marching straight off the ship onto a train, we were soon on our way to the dispersal camp at Chiseldon, which we reached about midnight. A good meal was served to us and, after a good night's rest in army huts, demobilisation began next morning.

— January 31st —

Demobilisation was so well organised that the whole procedure was over in an hour or so. At half past one I was on the train bound for home and, although still in khaki, was no longer 164684 Private Hoyte.

After changing at Cheltenham and again at Birmingham where, incidentally, the members of our party finally dispersed after a farewell drink in the buffet, I landed home at about eight-thirty in the evening with a far different outlook on life than when, nearly four years previously, I had been given my first regimental No. – 2987.

24

SUNDAY

Having depicted events in my army career which happened from day to day, I feel that the whole thing would hardly be complete without some reference to the fact of Sunday playing such a significant part in most of the big events, which the following will show.

— *1915* —

Sunday, June 27th – My last day as a civilian before joining up.
Sunday, November 14th – My last day in England before going overseas.

— *1916* —

Sunday, April 24th – The alarm was first sounded to call us out to reinforce the outposts which the Turks had overrun.

— *1917* —

Sunday, January 9th – Our victorious action at Rafah.
Sunday, July 29th – Arrived in Port Said for my first leave since leaving England.

— *1918* —

Sunday, March 31st – Received orders to proceed to France.
Sunday, April 7th – Left Palestine on first part of journey to France.
Sunday, May 26th – Sailed from Alexandria and torpedoed same night.
Sunday, June 30th – First day in France
Sunday, August 25th – Went up the line for the first time.
Sunday, September 15th – First day in the trenches.
Sunday, September 22nd – Last night in the trenches before proceeding on leave.

~ 1919 ~

Sunday, January 26th – Started home for demobilisation.
Sunday, February 2nd – First day back in civilian life.

If you enjoyed this book, you may also be interested in…

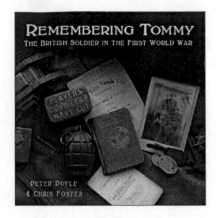

Remembering Tommy: The British Soldier in the First World War
PETER DOYLE & CHRIS FOSTER

Remembering Tommy pays tribute to the real-life British soldier of the Great War, from the moment of joining up to their final homecoming. Using original artefacts in historic settings, the men and their words are brought to life. Their personal possessions, mementos and photographs come together in a powerful tribute to the indomitable Tommy.

978 0 7524 7955 2

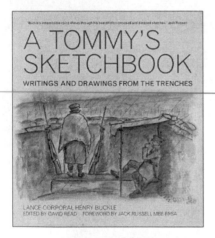

A Tommy's Sketchbook: Writings and Drawings from the Trenches
LANCE-CORPORAL HENRY BUCKLE, ED. DAVID READ

Henry Charles Buckle was an ordinary Tommy. During his time on the Ypres Salient he kept a diary and sketchbook. Contemporary colour images from the front are all too rare, and Henry's charming and naïve pictures are full of exquisite details and insights. From moving images of destruction to caricatures of his fellow soldiers and officers, this is a unique view of trench life.

978 0 7524 6605 7

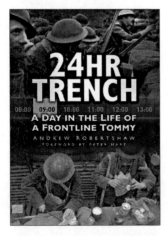

24hr Trench: A Day in the Life of a Frontline Tommy
ANDREW ROBERTSHAW

It is impossible to understand what it was like to live with the constant terror of enemy attack. Now, a group of soldiers recreate the trench experience using official war records and personal diaries. Hour-by-hour, the soldiers' lives are detailed in text, colour photographs and contemporary images, as well as interviews with those who took part.

978 0 7524 7667 4

Visit our website and discover thousands of other History Press books.

www.thehistorypress.co.uk

Lightning Source UK Ltd.
Milton Keynes UK
UKOW03f2218051113

220500UK00001B/10/P